W9-CTZ-610

Advance Praise for
Magic Time

"Is there anybody that Hawk Koch hasn't worked with? *Magic Time* should be required reading for three types of people. One, those starting in show business, two, those that have been in show business for a long time, and three, everyone else. Like every movie Hawk has made, *Magic Time* is a fascinating journey of self-identity. I love this book."

—**Mike Myers**, Actor, Writer, and Director

"*Magic Time* recounts what I remember about Hawk: someone who never took an opportunity for granted and worked hard to achieve success in his own right. Plus, he was a lot of the fun, and, as the book reflects, we had some memorable adventures."

—**Robert Redford**, Oscar-winning Actor and Director,
Founder of the Sundance Institute & Film Festival

"Hawk Koch is without a doubt one of the great Hollywood storytellers I've ever known. His adventures in the movie business are so funny and so incredible that I re-tell stories from his career more than ones from my own. And his own personal journey is as heartfelt as it gets."

—**Edward Norton**, Actor, Writer, and Director

"I can personally relate to this moving journey of a man learning to step out from under a father's shadow. But *Magic Time* is also filled with fun, surprising stories that only a deep insider could tell."

—**Jane Fonda**, Oscar-winning Actress, Bestselling Author

"I found the book profoundly moving, and insightful about not only the entertainment industry, but human nature. Bravo and congratulations!"

—**Gale Anne Hurd**, Producer, *The Terminator* and *The Walking Dead*

"This book is more than just a great Hollywood memoir. Hawk Koch shares his story with us in a funny, touching, and vulnerable way in contrast to the glitz and glamor of the show business life he leads. If you want to hear a story about what Hollywood is really like read this book. It's a winner."

—**Mark Gordon**, Producer of *Saving Private Ryan*, *Grey's Anatomy*, and *Criminal Minds*

"Some of my best times on set were when I could ask a million questions about how the actors, directors, and craftspeople brought movies to life. I asked Hawk a zillion questions about him, but they were really about his dad. This was before I learned a lesson from my daughter, who bitched to me once...or 100 times, 'No one ever asks me a question about me, they only want to know about you.' Later on, I was lucky enough to meet Hawk's dad. The pride of father to son, and from son to father, was always evident. In *Magic Time*, there's no mistaking it—Howard Koch and Hawk Koch are great reflections of each other. What's better than that?"

—**Whoopi Goldberg**, EGOT-winner, Actor, Host

"*Magic Time* is a wonderful, charming, heartbreaking, inspiring, redemptive story beautifully told. I am touched by it on so many levels, and Hawk's love of movies is infectious. Hawk is the guy that got us the p.g.a. Mark, and the animation producers the Oscar. He is the most dynamic, productive, and successful Academy leader I've seen in my lifetime. So, thanks, Hawk, for all you have done for us, for movies, and for the gift of this book."

—**Jim Morris**, President of Pixar Animation Studios

"Hawk Koch's climb up the proverbial ladder of success is by no means a mistake: not opting to be a dilettante, which he very well could have been, he did his homework, excelling in every facet...from the lowest up to the highest in the making of a film. His multitude of extraordinary incidents make for an inspirational, sometimes hilarious, behind-the-scenes, never-told, exciting read. His retelling of his incredulous experiences makes for a book to read and read again."

—**Robert Evans**, Producer, Bestselling Author of *The Kid Stays in the Picture*

"On one level, Hawk Koch has written a memoir on a life in Hollywood that will fascinate, inform and amuse you. His point of view is as close to ground zero as there is. On another level he has written an honest reflection on what it means to be a human being, on the long journey from the head to the heart. The skin of his tale describes America's dreams from post-WW II to now and the folks who made those dreams that shaped us. The bones are as old as Odysseus."

—**David Field**, Writer, Producer, and Former Studio Executive

"Not only is it a terrific movie book but Hawk unveils the personal difficulties of being the namesake of a very famous father and the nerve-racking ups and downs of life in Hollywood. A lively read of contemporary movie making from a key player."

—**Sid Ganis**, Producer, Former President of the Academy of Motion Picture Arts and Sciences

"Hawk Koch worked his way up from a location manager, to a 1st AD, to line producer, and then a full producer. He also ran a major production company. Hawk knows from the inside out how to truly produce a movie. This book will give you great insight and offer the secrets and skills of how to work with actors, writers, cinematographers, and especially directors. Hawk's complete knowledge about filmmaking makes this a must read for any producer."

—**Gary Lucchesi**, Producer, President of Lakeshore Entertainment

"Hawk brought a special type of leadership to the Academy while he was President because he viewed the film community as one, all equally important in the collective effort of getting a movie made. One of his great talents is making work fun. Optimistic, energetic, he moved the Academy forward while never losing sight of his first love: the movies and the people who make them. He gives readers an inspired and honest view of filmmaking and our filmmaking community."

—**Dawn Hudson**, CEO of the Academy of Motion Picture Arts and Sciences

MAGIC TIME

My Life in Hollywood

Hawk Koch

with Molly Jordan

POST Hill PRESS

A POST HILL PRESS BOOK

Magic Time:
My Life in Hollywood
© 2019 by Hawk Koch
All Rights Reserved

ISBN: 978-1-64293-302-4
ISBN (eBook): 978-1-64293-303-1

Cover art by Cody Corcoran
Cover Photo: Copyright © Academy of Motion Picture Arts and Sciences
Author Photo: Copyright © Motion Picture and Television Fund
Interior design and composition by Greg Johnson, Textbook Perfect

This is a work of nonfiction. All people, locations, events, and situations
are portrayed to the best of the author's memory.

PRESS

Post Hill Press
New York • Nashville
posthillpress.com

Published in the United States of America

For my children, Billy, Emily, and Robby,
and my grandchildren,
Payton, Cooper, Walker, Teddy, and Charlie,
in the hopes that someday you will come to understand
that my love for you is the river that runs
beneath every word in this book.

PROLOGUE

I grew up with all the privileges a kid has access to when he's fortunate enough to be born into a successful show business family. I have a lot to be grateful for, but as is true with everything else in life, what you see on the surface is only a portion of the whole story.

My father, Howard W. Koch, was a man that I—and everyone else in his orbit—cherished and admired. Dad was a famous movie producer in charge of Frank Sinatra's production company, then the head of Paramount Pictures, and ultimately president of the Academy of Motion Picture Arts and Sciences. No matter how high he soared professionally, he was always considered one of the most down-to-earth, kind, and thoughtful men in Hollywood. And the truth is, he was all that and more.

As my father's son, Howard W. Koch, Jr., it's true that there was no end to the privileges that came my way. Yet, being the namesake of a man who was a rare combination of highly successful and deeply beloved left me feeling like there was no way in the world I could ever measure up to him. Even so, that's exactly what I grew up believing I was supposed to do.

Because of his relationship to his father, Dad couldn't help me to wrestle with carrying the burden of his name. He wasn't personally communicative with his children, so he didn't understand the challenges I faced, and for a long time, neither did I. All my efforts to conceal that emptiness I felt inside were outwardly focused and fairly obvious.

My so-called defense systems worked well for a while, but as is always the case, eventually the truth catches up to you. When it caught up with me in 1995, I was about to turn fifty years old, and it led me to realize that I was falling apart.

Even though my professional life was humming along nicely, I didn't feel fulfilled by it. My kids had been hurt by the fact that I had brought too many women into their lives, and yet my love life was in shambles. In fact, if I had run a male-seeking-female personal ad, I would have had no choice but to admit: "Forty-nine-year-old, divorced father of three, unable to sustain meaningful relationship, seeking true love...again."

That explains why I was a complete wreck sitting across the lunch table from my good friend Gary Lucchesi not long after the most recent "love of my life" had broken up with me. Back then, Gary, former head of production at Paramount Pictures, and I were producing *Primal Fear* together.

He took one look at me right after a hug and a hello, and said, "Man, you look terrible." Then he laughed. That's Gary—he tells the truth in the most charming, youthful, and uplifting way, even when the truth hurts. He's a soul full of light and there's always an upside to being with him.

"It's been three weeks since Mary broke up with me, but the pain is excruciating, and I don't know what to do."

"Ah, I'm sorry, man." I knew he meant it.

I trusted Gary, which is what made it possible for me to add, "I'm desperate. If something doesn't change, like me, for example— if *I* don't change—I'm afraid I'm gonna end up a broken and lonely old man."

We sat together in the gravity of that truth until this epiphany dawned on me: "I need to give up searching for a soul mate and do some spiritual searching instead."

Gary—a good Catholic—lit up at the idea. "You're right. That's exactly what you need to do! Can you get bar mitzvahed for your fiftieth birthday?"

"I don't know. Are you serious?" I asked, dumbfounded.

"Yes, I'm dead serious, Howard. I've been to all your kids' bar and bat mitzvahs, and I've seen how each one has moved you to tears. I think this is just what you need, your own bar mitzvah. For your fiftieth birthday."

Gary was well aware that since neither of my parents were religious, I had never experienced that rite of passage most Jewish boys celebrate when they turn thirteen.

The hairs on the back of my neck jumped up and stood at attention—a sure sign something important had just been uttered. "Is that even possible?" I asked. "Can you get bar mitzvahed as an adult? And if you can, do you think I could actually do it for my birthday?"

Gary said, "I don't know, but why don't you find out? It's better than staying depressed."

And then with more enthusiasm than I'd felt in weeks, I said, "You know what? You're right. I am gonna find out."

I began my research that day and discovered it was possible to get bar mitzvahed at any age. Who knew? That heartening news set me off on the path to taking Gary's advice and finding just the right rabbi for the job. Before too long, I found my way to Rabbi Jonathan Omer-man.

I drove to his place on Wilshire Boulevard, arriving a little bit early for my appointment. His was the last one-story wooden cottage still standing between two towering office buildings in the middle of Los Angeles. I walked into that holy man's office, a blind squirrel utterly unaware that Rabbi Omer-man was about to provide me with a stash of acorns bountiful enough to keep me fed through all my winters to come.

The rabbi had a full head of tousled gray hair and was slightly stooped on metal crutches that braced his forearms. I would later learn he'd contracted polio during his twenty-six-year farming stint in Israel. This rabbi was a man of the earth, and something about that humbled me and set me at ease.

The room was noticeably dark, lit by only one dim lamp that had the odd effect of slowing me down, which, for me, is saying a lot.

When we sat down together, the rabbi asked me, in a slight British accent, why I'd come. He was easy to open up to, so I was able to tell him everything I could about what led me to him. I started by telling him that I came from a moviemaking family and that because I'd always loved going to the movies, I had followed in my father's footsteps to make them myself. I told him that my family was nonreligious and that I'd grown up in a home without an ounce of spirituality. I told him that I had moved my way up in the same industry as my father. Not only had I assisted directors like Roman Polanski, on *Chinatown* and *Rosemary's Baby,* and Sydney Pollack, on *The Way We Were,* but I'd run a couple of major production companies. By that time, I had been part of producing many movies, including *Heaven Can Wait, Gorky Park,* and *Wayne's World.* Despite those professional achievements, I told the rabbi that I still felt that I would never measure up to my father, that I would spend the rest of my life trying to crawl out from under his giant shadow. After all, he had received the highest level of recognition in our business: the Oscar. Not only had he received one himself, he'd also produced eight Oscar shows.

After talking with the rabbi for about thirty minutes, he said, "Let me ask you a difficult question: Who are you?"

That didn't seem so difficult to me, so I all too quickly answered, "Well, like I said, I'm a movie producer."

"No, who are you?" he asked again, making it obvious I didn't have a clue who I really was. I tried again, more certain I was on the right track this time, by saying, "Oh, I'm a father and I'm a son." He sighed and patiently asked with a genuine curiosity reminiscent of Alice's caterpillar when he pulled the hookah out of his mouth just long enough to inquire, "Whoooo are Youuuuuuuu?"

I slowed myself down another notch and thought about his question. It made me uncomfortable because I didn't know what to say. Self-conscious and grasping at the last remaining straw, I looked at the rabbi and ventured, "I am a Jewish man."

"Well, that's a start," he replied, which is precisely the moment I knew I was in deep trouble with this guy. Something told me he was going to have me looking at places in myself I had successfully avoided my entire life.

I struggled with every question the rabbi asked me during our meeting. Ultimately, I found myself wondering how a man as fortunate as me could be unable to answer the rabbi when he asked, "Who are you?"

Driving home, I told myself I was about to find out.

1

Growing up, we didn't take vacations. We only took *locations*. The three of us—me, my mother, and my older sister, Melinda—would visit my father on the sets of his movies.

In 1950, Dad was an assistant director working on studio films, We were on our way to Colorado for my first location visit. Because I'd always had bad allergies and asthma, we stopped to spend the night in Prescott, Arizona, advertised as "The best place in the country for people with allergies." I had the worst allergy attack of my life that night. Maybe I was nervous about visiting my dad.

By the next morning, I had recovered—we were driving out of Arizona, heading toward New Mexico. We were almost at the New Mexico border when a cop pulled my mother over.

"Do you know how fast you were driving, ma'am?" he asked.

"Yes, Officer," she said, trying to sound innocent. "The speed limit."

Just then my sister popped her head forward from the back seat to say to the officer, "She was not! I told her she was driving too fast."

"Thanks, Melinda. That's enough out of you," Mom scolded as we followed the cop back to a little Podunk town where she went before a judge and paid the astronomical sum of fifty bucks to get us out of trouble and out of town, back on the road to Colorado with Melinda having promised to keep her big mouth shut.

It was night by the time we finally arrived at a motel that had little individual cabins, all lined up in a row, like something you might see in a Laurel and Hardy movie. When my dad came into our cabin after work, my mom said to me, "Go get undressed so you can take a bath."

I did what I was told and went into the bathroom to get ready. There was a stand-alone claw-foot bathtub that was white with little black marbled lines running through it. When I looked inside the tub, I noticed the biggest spider I'd ever seen in my life. I didn't know it was a tarantula, but I ran screaming back to my mother, "There's a giant spider in the tub!"

I will never forget following my father into that bathroom. He carried his cowboy boot in his hand. The moment he hit the spider, hundreds of little baby tarantulas burst out of its stomach and flew all over that tub. It will not surprise you to learn that I have been an arachnophobe ever since. Maybe you just became one too. I still hope to use that memory in a movie one day.

I don't know if any of us slept that night, but the next morning after I got dressed, my mother said cheerily, "Today you're going to the set with your father." This idea and her delivery of it was intended to make me happy, but it scared me almost as much as the tarantula had because not only was I shy but I had never spent time alone with my dad and I didn't want to start now. Besides, I had no idea what a set was, having never been on one before.

"I don't want to go. I want to stay with you," I cried. And then I grabbed her dress and hid my face in it.

"C'mon, Legs. Get Little Howie in the car. I have to go to work," my dad insisted, calling my mother by his nickname for her.

Somehow, she managed to detach me from her skirt and get me in the car. I sat in the middle of the back seat, between my father and another man. It was early in the morning, the fog was thick, and there was little conversation. My crying was the only sound in the car. I felt intimidated and ashamed until the man next to me gently elbowed me and pointed out the window, a gesture that sent my eyes in the direction of his finger.

The beauty of the early Colorado morning shocked me because the fog had lifted and suddenly the mountains revealed themselves as if they had just yelled "Boo!" Startled out of my four-year-old's lousy mood, I found myself staring out the window, in awe of the pine trees, the stunning sky, and, as we approached our destination, the smoke on the horizon.

When the car stopped, I couldn't believe my eyes. The first thing I noticed were all the tepees, the feathered headdresses, and the horses exhaling great, visible clouds of breath exiting through their noses. There were wranglers and Indians gathered around the catering truck eating warm breakfast burritos from paper plates. My dad worked with cowboys and Indians? Whoa!

As if that wasn't enough magic for one kid to take in, while I was curiously looking inside one of the tepees, a big cowboy rode up to me on his horse and spoke directly—and only—to me.

"Howie, you ever been on a horse before?" he asked.

"No," I answered shyly, secretly enamored with the attention.

"You want to go for a ride?" the cowboy asked kindly.

"Yes!" I said, eyes wide with enthusiasm.

One of the men nearby lifted me up to the cowboy, who placed me in front of him on his saddle. With one hand on the reins, he took his other hand and held me close to him as we rode through the Indian village. I felt safe and much bigger than my age because I was visible to this man and I mattered. And I was on a horse, which I could not have known then would become a lifelong passion.

I didn't know or care that the cowboy was really Clark Gable, or that my father was the assistant director to "Wild Bill" Wellman on his film *Across the Wide Missouri*, or that Wellman had directed the first Oscar-winning film, *Wings*. I'd learn all that later. All I knew then was that I was on a big horse with a big cowboy and I felt more important than I had ever felt before.

After the ride, I was mesmerized by how they hit the slate, by watching the camera roll, and by feeling the camaraderie of everyone working together. Especially that.

Having my first horseback ride while in the grip of that man gave me my first taste of selfhood. Add to that the experience of being on a set with my dad—who, since he was a big deal, I got to be one too—and I was forever changed. I discovered what I loved that day. I never wanted to leave that magical place called a set, and I suppose in some ways I never have.

2

My family's love affair with moviemaking came courtesy of my paternal grandfather. Billy Koch was a character straight out of the movies. He and my grandmother Bea lived a chic, high-society life on the Upper West Side of New York City. Their lives included fancy handmade clothes and big-time friends, as well as governesses and private schools for their kids, my dad and his older sister, Lola.

But it wasn't always that way. Billy grew up in the tenements of New York City. A way out of that early poverty presented itself when it became obvious that he was practically a savant with numbers. By the time he was thirteen, Billy was working at the New York Stock Exchange, mainly writing numbers on the board and admiring the way people dressed in the Financial District.

See a picture of Billy as an adult and you can't help but notice how beautifully he dressed. You'd think he was an investment banker or maybe even a nattily dressed politician, but you'd be wrong. Billy parlayed his gift for numbers into a job that eventually led him to run the book at New York's Saratoga Race Course. Billy Koch was a bookie. It was a lucrative business. Saratoga Springs drew huge and wealthy crowds from New York City every summer. My grandfather was a well-connected man who knew the good guys like Al Jolson and Mayor Jimmy Walker, and the ones people thought of as bad because of their mob affiliations—guys like Frank Erickson and Frank Costello.

In fact, he had dinner with Bugsy Siegel the night before Siegel was murdered. Billy considered them all his friends.

In the early 1930s the state of New York decided it wanted to take a percentage of the betting pool instead of letting the bookmaker have it, so with one unfortunate enactment of a new law, bookmaking became illegal.

A guy like Billy wasn't going to be deterred by the inconvenience of a new law so he took matters into his own hands and decided to move his family from New York to the heart of West Hollywood, California. Bookmaking was illegal there too, but Billy figured he could be a little less visible, and besides, the milder weather would be better for his weak ticker.

It didn't take long for Billy's new business on Sunset Boulevard to become a thriving—albeit illegal—enterprise. His business was noticeably hot. The "hot" part was good news. The fact that it was "noticeable" wasn't so hot since his operation was now becoming visible to the cops, which could have meant trouble for him and for his more recognizable clients, including such Hollywood heavyweights as Darryl Zanuck and Louis B. Mayer.

In order to ensure the studio bigwigs their anonymity, it wasn't long before Grandpa Billy had an office on the lot, safely hidden behind the venerated gates of 20th Century Fox.

When my father was nineteen, Billy asked Darryl Zanuck to give his kid a job. Actually, the way my mother told it (she being the sole source of any information I ever received about my father) was that Billy, for reasons no one seems to know, frequently berated his son by telling him, "You're never gonna amount to anything, because you're nuthin' but a bum."

My mother said that Billy asked Zanuck to give his "bum" of a kid a job. Man, was he ever wrong.

In 1935, Zanuck hired my father to work in Fox's stock film library. My dad had set out to prove to his dad that he was anything but a bum. Unfortunately, Grandpa Billy never got to see how successful his son would become because he died of a stroke in 1948 when I was two, making me the heir to an unexamined father-son legacy that would have to live itself out between my father and me.

My grandmother Bea died a year after Billy. Everyone knew it was because her heart broke the moment he died. Unfortunately, I never got to know her either.

My mom, Ruth, was born in Los Angeles on September 28, 1919, to Joe and Sadie Pincus.

Joe and Sadie were both born on the Lower East Side of Manhattan. The passport of Joe's father, Morris Pincus, shows that he left Eastern Europe in the 1860s when Russian Jews were being persecuted and forced to flee.

Joe and Sadie were married in 1902. They moved to Los Angeles, where they were content to complete their family with their children Charlie and Rose, but seventeen years later, my mother was born. Sadie, convinced she was done with babies, was happy to defer most of Ruth's upbringing to the sixteen-year-old Rose.

The fact that my mother never really seemed to grow up and always maintained the nature and temperament of a little girl is likely due to the fact that she was—by a long shot—the baby in her family and was mostly raised by her teenaged sister.

My mother went to Los Angeles High School and then on to the University of Southern California (USC). Even though my dad wasn't in college, he attended a USC fraternity party where he met my seventeen-year-old mother. As the story goes, Mom was dancing when my father noticed her and admired her legs. Uncertain of her name when they met, he called her "Legs," a nickname that stuck.

My mother was so smitten with him that she dropped out of college to marry Dad, which is when she began her life as a devoted wife and, eventually, mother to me and my older sister, Melinda.

3

When I was born, my parents wanted to name me Billy, after my grandfather, even though in the Jewish tradition babies are only named after dead relatives. For reasons I will never understand, my parents decided instead to name me after my very alive father. The name bestowed upon me on December 14, 1945, was Howard W. Koch, Jr., but for quite a while, I was referred to simply as "Little Howie."

I was a happy kid, though it would surprise anyone who knows me to learn that as a toddler, I was shy and quiet.

Movies ranked right up there at the top of the list of things I loved. I loved watching them and getting to learn how they were made when I'd visit my dad's sets. He made what were called B movies, or "second features," sort of like the flip side of a hit record. The films I'd seen in theaters were small ones, like the ones my dad made. But for my tenth birthday, my mother took me and a handful of my friends to see *The Ten Commandments*. All of us got a Coke, some candy (I liked Milk Duds), and a bag of popcorn, the scent of which blasted your nose from the minute you entered the theater and plopped yourself down. That aroma of popcorn entered my system and had me hooked. To this day, I cannot see a movie without a bag of popcorn.

Once *The Ten Commandments* started, I was riveted. Never before had I seen anything the size or scope of Cecil B. DeMille's epic film.

It was so astonishingly real. I believed Moses was left in that little basket and that Egyptians had taken him and that the Red Sea really did part and that he went up to the top of Mt. Sinai and that he found a burning bush that talked. Wow! Not only did I fall in love with the movies on that day, but I knew that making them was what I wanted to do when I grew up. From then on, I saw every movie I could—old ones, classics, and new ones of every genre. I became an avid student of film. Still am.

My parents were no more political than they were religious. The entertainment industry was the altar at which they worshipped and served. Elijah didn't occupy the empty seat at our dinner table; the rotary-dial telephone did, it being the harbinger of all my dad's jobs. Everyone knows that the guest of honor sits to the right of the host and that is exactly the seat the exalted telephone occupied in our house. In the early days, it would sit like an entitled guest, right on top of the shiny mahogany dinner table, while its long, fraying, brown cord snaked its lazy path down to the floor.

Melinda is six and a half years older than me. We were World War II–bookend babies, she being born just before it and me just after. We shared the typical rivalry that happens when a baby brother enters the picture and appropriates all the attention from the one child who is still trying to get it from the busy parents.

I was my parents' favorite and Melinda…well, she was not. The difference boiled down to the fate of chromosomes. I was a boy in a (culturally if not religiously) Jewish family and was named after my father, who my mother considered a god. That made me god junior, while Melinda was considered "trouble" because of her contrary and spunky personality. That contrariness assured her she'd always be in trouble, but the spunkiness helped her tolerate and even thrive, no matter the punishment meted out or the challenges life threw at her.

Our parents left us to ourselves, and they expected us to discover our own interests, independent of them. We were raised as solo acts given second billing to our parents' starring roles.

My five-foot, two-inch mother had big hazel eyes that lit up with her quirky, girly laugh that you could hear a mile away.

She loved to dress up and go out with my father so she could have her two martinis in the midst of their rollicking social life. While she had plenty of friends and other interests, her preoccupation was my father. He was the sun around which her life orbited.

They were definitely a 1950s couple. Mom kept their dinner warm until he came home. Knowing he was on his way, she would go up to her room, redo her makeup and hair, change into a dress and heels, and wait for him to arrive. She was convinced he wanted to see the beautiful woman he married, not a tired mother feeding her kids, and she was probably right.

★ ★ ★

We moved to 1154 S. Camden Dr. when I was four. The new house was bigger, and just four houses outside the boundaries of Beverly Hills—a geographical detail that would soon come to matter a lot.

On Camden, the phone maintained its same honored seat just to the right of my father. I learned early on how much depended on whether your phone was ringing or not. Still does. But in those days, the days before cell phones, Crestview 1-7932 rang often.

I was home one night with a babysitter when the treasured telephone rang. Having grown to the ripe age of six, I had been taught exactly what to say when I answered it.

"Koch residence," I said proudly into the receiver of our 1950s telephone.

"Is your father home?" the unfamiliar, angry voice demanded.

"No, he's not. May I take a message?"

"Tell him he's a motherfucking, cocksucking Communist pig." Click.

Whoa! At six years old I wasn't used to hearing that language, especially applied to my father. I relayed the message, word for word, the moment my parents came home. I could see they were shaken, but

15

my father told me it was a mistake; they'd mistaken him for someone else with the same name. I knew something terrible had happened; I just didn't know what.

I would learn much later from my mother that Dad realized with that phone call that his name was being dangerously confused with another man named Howard Koch, the one who shared an Oscar for cowriting the movie *Casablanca*. That Howard Koch was investigated as part of Senator Joseph McCarthy's witch hunt, was denounced as a Communist, and was blacklisted by Hollywood.

Years later I realized just how important a call that was, since during the McCarthy era hundreds of Americans were accused of either being Communists themselves or, at the very least, sympathizers. Those who were accused became the subjects of aggressive investigations and interrogations. The Hollywood blacklist denied employment to screenwriters, actors, directors, musicians, and other entertainment professionals. Howard Koch suffered exactly that fate.

No wonder my dad was afraid of being confused with him. Dad was an assistant director making very little money at the time and was concerned he would lose his job. The day after that phone call came, my dad, by way of distinguishing himself from the other Howard Koch, officially added the "W" of his middle name, Winchel, and became known from then on as Howard *W.* Koch.

I was in awe of my father. He was a six-foot-tall, barrel-chested, blue-eyed man with a thick head of brown hair. When he was a kid, he severed a ligament in his right hand that left it permanently half closed, or half open depending on your point of view. This impairment made giving a firm handshake all the more valuable to my father, and he made sure I understood the importance of it. The other thing his injury did was keep him out of the service during the war. Unlike Vietnam, where none of us wanted to go, my dad always felt bad that he could not serve in the military during World War II.

I did not have either the entitlement or the courage to enter my father's orbit uninvited. It would never have occurred to me to direct his attention to me so that I could tell him a story about my day or talk to him about school, sports, or friends. And it never occurred to him either. He was a benevolent king, but not a hands-on dad.

I have no memory of him reading me a book, letting me sit in his lap, putting his arm around me, or ever giving me a kiss. I do remember one special time when he came into my room just as Jack LaLanne—a 1950s exercise star—happened to come on my television.

Looking at the TV and then back at me, Dad said, as if a lightbulb had just come on above his head, "Get up, Little Howie, let's do this!" I jumped up, surprised and happy for his visit, and then the two of us did jumping jacks and push-ups together. It didn't take too long for both of us to poop out and sit back down. It was in that exact moment of sitting down that Jack LaLanne suddenly looked into the camera and, as if speaking directly to us, said, "Oh no you don't, don't sit down! Keep going." My dad and I burst out laughing.

I cherish that memory because on that rare occasion the superhero was my dad.

From the time I was old enough to meet people, the first thing anyone ever said to me was how lucky I was to be my father's son. I remember making a run with Dad to Nate 'n Al's delicatessen to pick up some lox and bagels one Saturday morning. He always ran into someone he knew there. This day it happened to be his pal Joel Freeman.

"Hey, Howard, how are ya doin'?" Joel said, clearly happy to see my dad. Always polite, Dad said, "Terrific, Joel. Have you ever met my son, Little Howie?"

Joel, without hesitating even a beat, said to me, "You must be so proud. Do you know what a wonderful man your father is? Everybody loves him." Then his eyes returned to my father. It seemed like there was something I was supposed to do in that moment; it's just that I didn't know quite what. I felt awkward and self-conscious.

Because some version of this event happened over and over again (and in fact still does nearly twenty years after my father's death), I eventually did learn what it was I was supposed to do. I learned to expect that anyone who was meeting me for the first time, upon hearing my name, would be instantly transported to a fond memory they had of my father. Their enchantment was so immediate and so complete that they would be compelled to share their story of a kindness he had bestowed upon them. Anyone else around them—like me, for example—didn't exist. Over time, I learned that I was not a young boy (or even the grown man I became) in these moments, but a blank screen onto which they could project their thoughts and glowing reflections about my father. I learned I was invisible.

4

In 1952 my dad got an offer from producer Aubrey Schenck to partner with him in a production company. Their Bel-Air Productions was a big step up the movie-business ladder for Dad. They made a deal with United Artists, and over the next seven years produced lots of second features, a couple of which Dad directed. They worked in LA and places like Kanab, Utah, and Cañon City, Colorado.

Since the movies they made were mainly B movies, their budgets were bare bones. One summer they made a French Foreign Legion action movie on the sand dunes of Yuma, Arizona. Their down-and-dirty budget only allowed them fifty costumes, half for the legionnaires and half for the Arabs, and twenty-five horses.

High on the right side of the sand dune stood a line of twenty-five Arab riders atop their horses. They filmed that line from a couple of different angles, so it looked like there were more than seventy-five or one hundred of them.

When the director yelled, "Action," those twenty-five Arabs came roaring down the hill on their horses with their scimitars raised high above their heads. When they reached the bottom and the director yelled, "Cut," those twenty-five men took off their Arab costumes to reveal French Foreign Legion outfits underneath. The wardrobe man ran out at that point and handed out twenty-five Foreign Legion hats to repeat the scene from their perspective. I learned a lot about making movies on a tiny budget.

In 1957 my dad directed a movie called *The Girl in Black Stockings,* a murder mystery shot in Kanab, Utah. Kanab was known as Utah's "Little Hollywood" because of all the films shot there in the '50s, plenty of which were made by my dad and Aubrey.

Mom and I were having another location visit with him just as he was finishing up the film. Everyone, including us, stayed at Parry Lodge, a hotel founded by the Parry brothers in 1931. It's still there to this day.

The wrap party for *The Girl in Black Stockings* was held right there at the Lodge, and I got to go. I remember meeting Anne Bancroft, a new actress everyone was excited about. She was nice, but the one I was more eager to meet was Mamie Van Doren. She looked like Marilyn Monroe, and I was just beginning to appreciate the wonderful effects a sexy and zaftig woman like Mamie could have on an almost twelve-year-old kid like me. Mamie was a platinum blonde, with hair that undulated around her. When she walked on the set, I noticed how every man on the crew stopped what they were doing to stare at her. The heat from her steamy sexuality was impossible to ignore. I think she pushed me right over the brink into puberty when she danced with me at the wrap party that night.

The fact that I was eye level to Mamie's breasts made dancing with her an especially life-altering moment. From that night on, girls became my full-time interest, and dancing with them, I soon learned, was a great way to get close to them.

When I was in sixth, seventh, and eighth grades, there were dances every Friday night at the local YMCA. I had two or three girlfriends back then, one of whom was Louise, still my friend today. Louise and I won every dance contest. Another one of my dance-partner girlfriends was Rita Litter. When my dad made a movie called *Bop Girl Goes Calypso,* Rita and I danced together in a scene.

Dad had me get a bunch of kids together for that dance. Everyone thought he was cool because not only did he make movies but now he was making one *they* got to be in. That gave me a little bit of peripheral cool because he was my dad, even though nobody would have guessed that we rarely interacted. I never thought anything about that, really, because I didn't know anything else, until one day when I went to visit my best friend Robbie and saw him in the living room talking to his mom and stepdad, Sumner Long.

At first, I thought maybe he was getting in trouble for something, but it didn't take long to figure out they were just talking. "Oh, hi, Howie, come on in and join us," Sumner encouraged. I always felt at ease around him because whenever I saw him, he'd be sitting in his big cushy rocking chair, completely relaxed, rhythmically lighting and tamping down his pipe tobacco, a habit that had a mesmerizing effect on me. Because Robbie called his mom by her name, Beulah, and his stepdad Sumner, so did I.

"Thanks, Sumner," I said stepping into the living room, feeling a mix of awkwardness and curiosity about what they were all doing together.

As if reading my mind, Beulah said, "We're just chatting. What's new with you, Howie?"

What? They were just talking to one another for no reason? That surprised me. And on top of that, having an adult ask me a personal question because they were interested in my answer was such unfamiliar territory that at first I didn't have a clue how to respond.

Even though I was a little thrown, I felt their genuine curiosity and invitation to join their conversation. Besides, I was eager to tell someone what had happened to me recently.

Sitting down I said, "Well, a few nights ago I woke up in the middle of the night. That's weird for me, but since I was awake, I turned on the radio to listen for a little while. It turned out the Russians had just launched Sputnik into outer space. Isn't that amazing?"

A lively discussion followed as we all talked about how close the United States might be to launching our own satellite, but what really blew me away was the fact that here were two parents talking to me and their son solely because they wanted to hear what was on our minds.

It struck me at that moment that *that's* what cool was; cool was when your parents were taking interest in you and wanting to know what you thought about things. I had every privilege in the world, but that day I became aware of something I didn't have.

In my house, if we were all together as a family, say, one of the rare times Melinda and I were having dinner with our parents, my father presided over the table. He was a great storyteller. He'd regale us with a tale about what the next movie would be or what "that stupid sonofabitch I'm working with" did, and Melinda and I would be held in the palm of his hand. Sometimes he'd pass along a morality lesson. I remember one such night when Mom was telling Dad about a woman who would be joining her as the fourth in their golf game, saying, "I've heard she cheats and already I don't like her."

Dad said, "You don't like her, but you haven't met her. It reminds me of a story Danny Thomas tells that is a good lesson.

"Picture this, it's years ago—before freeways—and a guy is driving to Palm Springs, right? All of a sudden, he's got a flat tire and has to pull off to the side of the road. He thinks to himself, 'No big deal. I'm going to Palm Springs. Yeah, baby!' The guy opens the trunk, takes the spare out, puts it on the ground, and searches for the jack. 'Hmm, no jack. Now what am I gonna do?' He starts to flag down someone who maybe has a jack. Nobody stops. He thinks, 'All right, maybe I'll walk a little bit. Somebody will pick me up.' He walks a little bit and sees a big sign: 'Joe's Service Station. Brand new. Best station in all of Palm Springs. Five miles.' He thinks, 'Oh great, I'll head there. Somebody will give me a ride, they'll have a jack at Joe's. Joe himself will drive me back, put the tire on, and man, I'll be in Palm Springs in no time.'

"As he starts to walk a little farther, still no one is picking him up, and now it starts to get windy. Really windy. Sand is blowing in his face. All of a sudden, he sees dark clouds over the mountain. Then he sees another sign that says, 'Joe's brand-new service station. Come to Joe's.' He figures, 'Ahh, it's just another few miles. I'll keep walking and somebody will pick me up. Maybe Joe will charge me a couple of bucks for the jack but so what. They'll take me back, and there won't be a problem.'

"The guy walks a bit farther, and wouldn't you know it, it starts to rain. Now he's got the sand in his face, and it's raining, his hair is a mess, he wasn't prepared for this—and still nobody is picking him up. He keeps walking, but he's sopping wet. He sees the sign: 'Come to Joe's, greatest service station.' He thinks to himself, 'Jesus, the guy's gonna charge me ten bucks, and now I'm gonna have to take a taxi back. What kind of guy is this Joe? Nobody's picking me up. What if I have to buy a jack?' He's walking a bit farther and now it's pouring rain and he is a total mess. He's freezing, it's cold, and he sees the sign: '1/4 of a mile. Joe's Service Station. Come on in! Best service in all of Palm Springs.' He's walking, and he's exhausted, and he's sopping wet, and he says, 'The sonofabitch is gonna charge me twenty-five bucks just for a fucking jack? And I'm gonna have to get a taxi. And the taxi cab won't help me change the tire. What a fuckin' mess!' And finally, there it is: Joe's garage. It's brand spanking new. It's beautiful. He walks in and opens the door to the service station manager, and he says, 'Are you Joe?' The guy couldn't have been more cordial when he says, 'Yes, that's me. How can I help you?' And our tired, sandy, sopping wet guy says, 'You can take your fuckin' jack and your fuckin' best service station and go shove it up your ass. I don't want anything to do with you!' And then he left."

We all laughed, but Dad wasn't finished because then he added the moral of the story by looking Mom, Melinda, and me straight in the eyes and saying, "So don't you ever judge, don't assume you know something until you know something. You get it? Don't do the jack story."

Both Mom and Melinda, proud of themselves, said, "You bet. I get it."

Not to be excluded I said, "I do too!" although I wasn't entirely sure I did.

5

My parents wanted me to have a better education than what they felt I could get within the Los Angeles City School District. Because we lived four houses outside the city limit, I wasn't allowed to attend the higher quality Beverly Hills schools. But I got a lucky break because my dad filmed a portion of a movie at the high school, and in the permitting process had developed a relationship with the superintendent of the school system. Dad pulled the first of many strings he would pull by getting me into fifth grade at the Horace Mann School in Beverly Hills.

It's scary being the new kid in a school where everyone has already made their friends because they've been together for years. Luckily, two boys, Robbie Long and Bobby Perlberg, took me under their wing, and instantly I felt like I belonged.

There was no question that I was going to sign up and try out for Beverly Hills Little League. My parents were aware of my plan, but I didn't have any expectation that either of them would accompany me. All my friends and I were hoping to be on the same team, but first, we had to try out.

When the chilly Saturday morning in February arrived, I rode my bicycle the five minutes to Roxbury Park and laid my bike on the ground—this was the '50s, and we didn't use locks. I ran to sign myself up and then proceeded to wait with my friends while the coach called one name after another. When it was my turn, I went out to show them what I could do, fielding grounders and shagging fly balls. All the rest of the kids sat and waited for their turn to come up.

After only a few balls, I heard a voice over the loudspeaker say my name. "Howard Koch, Jr., please come to the registration table."

When I got there, in front of all the other kids, the coach announced, "I'm sorry, but you can't try out, Howard. You can't be on a team because you don't live in the city of Beverly Hills."

I could feel the heat of shame instantly rise to burn my face. Until that moment, I had no idea that I could be punished so drastically simply because our house was four houses outside the Beverly Hills city limits. I stared down at my feet, hoping my shame wouldn't show. I felt as if everyone was looking at me like something was wrong with me—and there was: I couldn't play.

My friends had no idea what to say or do. They were just excited to make the team themselves, so they all looked down at their feet, just as I was doing, and scuffed some dirt with their cleated shoes while the awkwardness grew. The next move was up to me. I steeled myself and walked over to pick up my bike. I rode home deeply embarrassed and hurt, wondering how I was going to tell my parents what had happened.

I came home to an empty house and immediately went up to my room. When my parents eventually came home, they never asked how the tryout went, and I never told them.

★ ★ ★

When I was thirteen, I ended up in the Beverly Hills Pony League, which you play at thirteen and fourteen years old. They knew I was out-of-district, but in Pony League those four houses didn't matter because a lot fewer kids tried out and they needed players.

Our team was called the Pirates, and our pitcher was also one of my best friends. His name was Jim Palmer. Jim was so much better than anybody else in the whole Pony League. He went on to pitch for the Baltimore Orioles, and today is in the Baseball Hall of Fame.

When I was fourteen, I was on the Athletics, and our coach was Eddie Hoffman. We had sliding drills at one of our early practices, and I was helping Eddie teach the thirteen-year-olds how to do a hook slide into second base. Determined to give it my all during my demonstration, I ran as fast as I possibly could and threw myself into the slide, but the cleat below my left big toe caught in the dirt and snapped. I was lying on the ground in excruciating pain and couldn't get up. Eddie called my parents.

I was relieved when before too long my mother came running to me. She was comforting and reassuring. "It's gonna be okay, Howie. I promise. Dad's on his way." My dad arrived just a bit later, but instead of coming directly to me, he stopped where the rest of the team was hanging out. I could overhear him telling them an exciting story about the scene he was directing when he'd gotten the call to come to the park. I knew they were falling in love with him.

Eventually, they got me into the back of our family station wagon and drove me to an orthopedist's office. When the X-rays revealed I had broken both my tibia and fibula, I was taken by ambulance to Cedars of Lebanon Hospital. The next morning, I had an operation to repair the bones in my leg. I was in an up-to-my-groin cast for almost three months, all of which I spent lying around watching movies on TV while perfecting the fine art of eating hamburgers.

The following Friday was our first game of the season. Even though I was on crutches with a cast, there was no way I was going to miss that first game.

My mom drove me to the park. I hobbled as fast as I could out to the bleachers. Some of my teammates came by to say hi. One of them, Rick Podell, said, "Hi, Howard. Glad you're here. Your dad is so bitchin', telling us all those stories about the TV show he's directing. I wish my dad was like him."

Neither of us knew then that twenty-six years later Rick and his partner would write a screenplay called *Nothing in Common*, which I would shepherd into a film after becoming a movie producer myself.

I took in Rick's remark. I did feel special having a dad other kids thought was cool, but at the same time, their mentioning it gave me a palpable sense of emptiness. I was beginning to become aware of a hole developing inside myself, and I didn't like it. The feeling was so uncomfortable that I buried it as fast as it arose.

★ ★ ★

In 1960, my dad was offered two jobs in the same week. The first was to become partners with Quinn Martin, the producer of such popular television shows as *The Fugitive* and *The FBI*. Despite what a great offer that was, the second was one he couldn't refuse: Frank Sinatra had called.

Hollywood is a small town. Your reputation is everything, and my father's was stellar. When he was being considered for the job, his first meeting was with Mickey Rudin, Frank's attorney. After that went well, he met with Frank, who liked my father immediately and, as was his way, hired Dad on the spot to run his movie company.

My dad went from having a nice career as a producer of B movies and a director of TV shows, to running the movie company of the biggest star of the day. Suddenly everyone knew who Howard W. Koch was. With all the changes and the hoopla this move brought, my father never changed who he was, how he saw himself, or how he treated people. He stayed humble and kind, generous and professional.

In doing his due diligence on Frank, my dad found that most people who had worked for him tended to socialize with him outside of work, wanting to be his friend. Most of those people ended up getting fired. Dad decided he would skip the friendship and would stick to a professional relationship only. That plan turned out to be a wise one.

★ ★ ★

In 1958 my sister and I were sharing a hotel room in New York City while my dad was making a movie there, and Melinda got set up on a date with a man named Ben Stanton. I was supposed to be asleep when she got back, but I remember listening to them saying good night at the door when Ben dropped her off.

That was the night Melinda fell in love, and by the time she was twenty, she had married Ben. After they married, Melinda and Ben lived in Fort Lee, New Jersey, and by August of 1961, they had their first child, Wendy Nan Stanton.

In the summer of 1961, between my sophomore and junior years at Beverly High, a bunch of my friends and I decided to make a movie. We called it *The Cop's Ketchup*. I directed it. We filmed it on a borrowed 8 mm camera and wrote, acted, and edited it ourselves over the course of a weekend. It was the first time I got to be a producer/director, and I loved every minute of the experience. Even if it was just a high school lark, I was aware that being on our makeshift set felt like home to me.

When it was ready, we screened *The Cop's Ketchup* for our families and friends. It was a big hit. Everyone's enthusiastic response only added to my conviction that I wanted more moviemaking in my life.

6

As head of Frank's company, Dad was now making enough money so that he and my mom could finally head north to live within the much-vaunted Beverly Hills city limits. Right after my high school graduation, they bought a house on North Crescent Drive, where they would live for the rest of their lives. Despite the move, and even though I was headed to college at UCLA, I had already been branded out-of-district, a stigma that on some level I still carry deep in my bones.

★　★　★

One of the first things I did when I started UCLA in 1963 was rush the ZBT fraternity. I pledged, got in, and had a ball. My big brother at ZBT was Robert Shapiro, who, long after the innocence of those days had left us, would represent O. J. Simpson in his murder trial.

The homecoming football game was November 22 of my freshman year, and the ZBTs were making a float with the Kappa sorority. They were beautiful, dark-haired girls who all looked like Natalie Wood to me, and seemed just as inaccessible and, therefore, incredibly alluring.

As a pledge, I was sent to the Crown Zellerbach in downtown LA to get more crepe paper for the float. I left around ten in the morning and about an hour later was standing at the counter with my arms full of crepe paper, when the music I'd been ignoring on the store radio was interrupted for a special bulletin. President Kennedy had been shot in Dallas.

The man behind the counter and I looked at each other and gasped. There were no words exchanged between us, just a look of stunned disbelief. I paid the bill, a different person from the kid who'd walked in to buy crepe paper for a college fraternity float. I threw the paper in the back of my car, got inside, turned on the radio, and drove.

When I heard the words that President Kennedy was dead, I pulled onto the shoulder, turned off my engine, and cried like I hadn't in a long, long time—maybe ever. I wasn't the only one. The freeway looked like I imagined the Red Sea must have looked after Moses parted it because there were cars along both sides of the road with shocked and grieving drivers trying to absorb the news.

When I got back to UCLA, everything was quiet and empty but for the loudspeaker coming from the quad. I arrived there to find thousands of students sitting on the ground crying, comforting one another, and listening to the news.

The world of being an innocent freshman, pledging a fraternity, and busying myself with card games and float decorating came to an abrupt end.

I didn't live on campus, so eventually, I drove back to my parents' house. I went straight upstairs and locked myself in my room for several days, depressed and lost.

Hibernating in my room, I watched the shooting of Lee Harvey Oswald replayed. With his murder, we'd be forever deprived of the real story behind JFK's assassination. By the time I emerged I knew one thing: I did not want to go back to college.

★ ★ ★

One evening that winter, my parents were having a dinner party, and I found myself talking to an Englishman named Harold Davison, a booking agent who lived in London. He'd booked and was responsible for bringing Frank Sinatra into the Royal Albert Hall. Harold dazzled me with stories about managing American and English rock groups in London. As he was talking to me, I asked him, "Do you think I could have a job in England?"

To my surprise, he didn't hesitate and said, "Sure."

"Are you serious?" I asked.

"Of course I'm serious." When he said that, he had done the equivalent of handing me a purpose, along with a road map. I was going to London to work in the music industry.

★ ★ ★

Early in 1964, my parents were in Italy because my dad was producing *Von Ryan's Express* for Frank, and some of it was being shot in Rome. I traveled there on my way to my job in London.

While I was there, Dad got a call to meet with the owners of Paramount Pictures. They offered him a job as head of production. My mother told me about it and said, "Dad is scared stiff to tell Frank for fear of how he might react." I was sitting on a ladder outside Frank's dressing room on the set when Dad walked in to tell him. I felt nervous too, knowing a bit about Frank's temper.

Frank was his own version of Jekyll and Hyde. One minute he was warm and magnetic and you just fell in love with him, but then suddenly he'd turn and would do something that was intended to—and usually did—scare the crap right out of you.

I was happy when my dad came out of his meeting looking relieved. He told my mom and me that Frank thought it was "Fucking terrific they offered you the job. It just shows that I know who to fucking hire. Go be the head of Paramount. We'll make movies over there."

And that's exactly what Dad did: after four years of running Frank's company, he left Rome and went home to run Paramount Pictures. I flew to London with my mother, where she helped me find a flat so I could be ready to work for Harold Davison.

I remember being confronted with a whole new sense of loneliness when she flew home. Suddenly I was by myself in London with not an ounce of street smarts; this was a whole new and unfamiliar level of independence. I was scared, but I had made the decision to go and knew I was going to have to figure it out. The next morning, I got on the number six bus and rode it from Edgware Road to Piccadilly, to the office where I worked for the next several months.

Since everyone was older than me and fully ensconced in their own worlds, I did not have a social life or friends. I'd go to work alone and come home alone. On the weekends, I'd walk to Hyde Park and hang out at Speakers' Corner, where people had been coming to talk, debate, and listen for more than a hundred years. I experienced a depth of desolation I had never known before.

★ ★ ★

One night after I'd been in London for several months, I was invited to a Yom Kippur break-fast being hosted by a family friend, Charles Schneer, a well-known film producer. When I sat down at the table, I turned to the man seated next to me, extended my hand, and said, "Hi. I'm Howard Koch."

When he said, "That's funny, so am I!" my heart jumped right up into my throat, leaving me speechless.

Oh, my God, I thought, completely flummoxed, it's him. It's the other Howard Koch!

This was the man I had allowed myself to both fear and hate from the time that phone call came when I was six years old. I decided long before that I could never like or respect a man who caused my dad such worry and now he was sitting right next to me.

Partly because that phone call had made such an impression on me, I became fascinated by the dark period of the McCarthy era as I grew older. I had sympathized with those people who were expected to name names, and with those who were blacklisted and unable to work. I became convinced of how unfair it was that the careers of most of the people McCarthy went after were ruined. In spite of my convictions, I continued to hold a hefty resentment toward the other Howard Koch. The importance of that "W" in my father's name was ingrained in me and he always made sure that whenever I talked about him or told someone his name, I never forgot to add that distinguishing W.

What was I going to do now that the infamous man without the "W" was sitting right next to me? My immediate reaction was to recoil, but once I started to talk to him I learned one of my biggest personal lessons: I, a young man who considered himself open-minded and fair, had held a glaring grudge for many years toward a man I'd never met.

He made it easy for me to encounter this part of myself because he was kind and compassionate.

"Sharing the same name as me must have been quite challenging for your dad," he said sincerely.

"Yes, it was." I told him about the phone call when I was six and how Dad had added his middle initial so the two of them would not get mistaken for one another.

Howard Koch, who cowrote the Oscar-winning classic *Casablanca*, turned out to be a gentleman who had been—and still was—clearly passionate about social justice. He was a good human being who suffered for carrying the burden of his convictions, which he assured me had nothing to do with being a Communist.

Because he pled the fifth instead of admitting to being a Communist, he was forced to leave his country. That meant that in spite of his vast talent as a writer, he was forced to move himself and his family to England and work under a pseudonym.

America was frightened of progressive politics (then as now), just as I was frightened of what I had conjured up about this man my entire life.

"Ya see, Howie," I could practically hear my dad whispering in my ear, "don't let your fear make you repeat the jack story." For the first time in my life, I finally understood the moral of that tale.

7

Within a few weeks of starting my job in London, Harold told me about Johnny, a man in his forties who used to pick up American rock 'n' roll acts for him when they'd fly into Heathrow. Harold thought that since most of the rockers were closer to my age, I should greet them at the airport instead. So I did. I started picking them up, getting them to their hotels, their TV shows, or their concert venues, and then taking them to the Ad Lib, the best discotheque in London.

This was exciting to me and not just because of the proximity I had to the rock stars, although that was certainly a part of it. I was making hardly any money—twelve pounds a week—and had zero social life. I'd eat a Wimpy burger on my way home and then spend the rest of the night by myself. Not only was my social life about to change, but I had an expense account!

The first person I picked up was Lesley Gore. Harold sent me with a driver in a great old Bentley to pick up her, her mother, and her music producer, Quincy Jones. I was as excited as I was nervous standing there at Heathrow, waiting and holding up a sign for her. I knew her music so well. I loved "It's My Party."

I checked them into the Mayfair Hotel, got them upstairs, and told them that we were going to the Ad Lib that night. It was exclusive. The only people who could get in were rock stars, movie stars, and their entourages. I had heard about it, but until the promotion, I didn't stand a chance of getting into the hottest place in London.

By this time in 1964, the Beatles had already performed on *The Ed Sullivan Show*, sparking the cultural phenomenon that had teenagers swooning over British rock acts, and every other aspect of British culture as well. The Beatles were number one, but right behind them were the Dave Clark Five, the Kinks, the Rolling Stones, Herman's Hermits, the Hollies, and Peter and Gordon. And they all hung out at the Ad Lib.

The discotheque was down a side street off Leicester Square. You had to take a freight elevator up to the top floor. Since I was chaperoning Lesley, her mother, and Quincy, I didn't tell them—and hoped my excitement didn't reveal—that it was my first time there as well.

We walked into a dark room that had little tables all over the place. There was a dance floor to the left of the tables and behind the dance floor stood a hollowed-out piano where Teddy, the DJ, spun forty-fives. People danced and drank and nibbled on Chinese hors d'oeuvres. There was a second room—deeper inside the club—full of booths and more tables.

Everybody there was a star.

When Lesley walked in, Dusty Springfield came up to say hello.

I was so excited, my stomach was turning somersaults, and all the while I was trying to maintain my professional cool so I could properly tend to Lesley and her group.

Man, if my friends could only see me now, I thought.

The second day of their stay, Lesley invited me up to their suite. We were alone, and she was standing by the fireplace. She seemed— not nervous exactly—but vulnerable when she said, "I know you like my songs. I just recorded this one that hasn't been released yet, but I'd love to know what you think."

Then she pressed the button on the tape recorder sitting on top of the mantel and played "You Don't Own Me."

That's right, "You Don't Own Me," in my opinion her best song. I was entirely blown away by it and didn't hesitate to tell her so.

"Wow, not only is it fantastic; it's powerful! You know I'm a big fan of your music—I told you that—but this one is different. This one is deep. I absolutely love it!"

I couldn't believe that Lesley Gore, even though she was my generational peer and a huge pop star, was asking me my opinion about her music. Me!

Decades later, I was attending an annual charity event in Los Angeles and Lesley, who had become a great jazz and blues artist by then, was there to perform. We were genuinely excited to see one another, each of us now in our forties, with a lot of water having passed under our respective bridges. Life may have changed us, but our affection for one another remained the same.

★ ★ ★

The next group I got to pick up was the Ronettes. They were three young girls looking for a good time. And they found one.

I took them to their hotel, this time the Strand Palace Hotel on the Strand, to get settled and then to the discotheque. Coming with Lesley Gore was one thing, but escorting the Ronettes caused a whole other stir with the British stars who couldn't wait to meet them since "Be My Baby" was such a huge hit.

I sat with them at one of the little tables and was as excited as they were when one of them would notice a British rock star.

"Look, there's fucking John Lennon!" twenty-one-year-old Veronica Bennett, who was known as Ronnie (and would later marry Phil Spector) yelled, pointing excitedly, not caring a whit who noticed or heard. Ronnie loved to have fun.

All our jaws dropped when Ringo Starr came up and asked Ronnie to dance. Eighteen-year-old Nedra Talley, another of the Ronettes, wasn't going to miss out on being near that fire, so to my surprise, she turned to me and said, "Hey, Howard, wanna dance?"

"Yes!" I said.

We walked out and managed to maneuver ourselves near Ringo and Ronnie, and then both Nedra and I proceeded to let it all go. When the song was over, Ronnie leaned over to me and said, "Howard, you dance like a fucking n*****."

To hear that from Ronnie Bennett was by far the highest compliment I'd ever received.

***

Harold Davison, my boss, was the co-owner, along with Dave Clark, of the band the Dave Clark Five. In the summer of 1964, the DC5 had actually sold more records than the Beatles, though that had changed by the fall.

Harold told me that Dave and the boys had an upcoming three-month US and Canadian tour and I was to be one of their roadies.

We did forty-eight cities in fifty-two days in the United States and Canada. I spent my nineteenth birthday in Memphis, Tennessee, with Dave and the boys.

Our tour was to start in New York City with an appearance on *The Ed Sullivan Show*. When we arrived at the airport, there weren't nearly as many kids as we anticipated, or as had shown up for the Beatles. Naturally, this disappointed all of us, but especially Harold.

He called from London to say, "We need more press coverage because we're not selling out the venues. We've got to get some great PR."

The next day, the day of *The Ed Sullivan Show*, I was sitting shotgun in the limousine and the boys were in the back. Two or three other limousines were behind us. I'd been wracking my brain—as I'm sure we all had—about how to ratchet up the energy.

There were crowds of fans lining Fifty-Third Street, standing behind blue police barricades. I suddenly thought, what if our limousine "accidentally" stopped about two hundred feet before the entrance to the theater? I bet those kids would knock down the barricades and run toward the limo to get near the boys.

There were all kinds of press people outside with their cameras ready, and I figured this "accident" would give them something exciting to shoot. I whispered to the driver who owned the limousine company, "Why don't you turn the engine off a couple hundred feet before the entrance?"

He said, "But they might hurt my car if they jump over those barricades."

I did not say that jumping the barricade was exactly what I hoped would happen, since it would bring us just the attention we needed. But I assured him quietly that we'd take care of any damage to his limo.

"Are you sure?" he asked.

"Absolutely," and I meant it.

As we got to the spot far enough from the entrance, but close enough to the press, I quietly told the driver to turn off the engine. The kids noticed the second we stalled and started leaping over the barricades and sprinting toward the limo. They were waving and crying, and all the press people suddenly started snapping photos, capturing the whole "mob scene."

After the photos hit the wires across the United States, our ticket sales increased. And there you have my first, and probably only, PR success.

I was busy now—flying in, setting up, organizing press conferences, and arranging cocktail parties with city fathers and their DC5-crazed daughters. There was no time to be lonely anymore. It was an amazing opportunity for me, some of which I got to share with my friends when we'd play in a city near their college campuses.

I would regale my friends with stories about the girls who were crazy about anyone British or who had anything to do with the Dave Clark Five. Every girl in America wanted to be with Paul McCartney or Dave Clark, and if they couldn't be with one of them, then they wanted to be with the manager, or even a mere roadie like me.

We played with Little Anthony and the Imperials. We played with the Shirelles. In St. Louis we played with Chuck Berry, and in Birmingham, Alabama, with Roy Orbison.

While we were setting up in Birmingham and had an hour or two before the concert, I was walking around the arena looking for a bathroom. When I saw the men's room sign, I walked in quickly to relieve myself. While standing there, an African American man walked in and gave me a startled and strange what-are-you-doing-here look.

I left quickly and stepped outside where I noticed a Caucasian man looking at me just as strangely. I followed his eyes on their route up above where I had seen the bathroom sign, and only then noticed the word "Colored" above the word "Men."

After this experience in the "Colored Only" men's room, my stomach turned, and I felt a flood of emotions, but it was the upwelling of anger that surprised me even more than the sadness that surged. True to my development as a loner, I did not discuss this experience with anyone. I tucked it safely inside myself where it has continued to inform my beliefs and my politics.

I couldn't have been more excited that Roy Orbison would be opening. In the movie *Swimming to Cambodia,* Spalding Gray writes about what he describes as a perfect moment. I will never forget witnessing Roy Orbison walk out on the stage with his Fender Stratocaster to the screaming din of his idolizing fans. When he held up his hands to hush them, the audience became immediately and utterly silent. When he put his hands back on his guitar and finally began the first notes of "Only the Lonely," this music-loving teenager was in a perfect moment.

It must have been equally true for the fans because they went entirely nuts and sustained their screaming until the last note of the last encore of his huge hit "Pretty Woman" had been played.

We had a typical pattern of how we got paid at every venue: the road manager Rick or I, or sometimes both of us, would go to the promoter at intermission to pick up either a cashier's check or cash, prior to Dave and the boys going on. If we didn't come back to their dressing room with money in hand, they wouldn't go on. The promoters always gave us a security detail to make sure we got back safely.

Rick and I knew the contract, and we'd counted the house in Birmingham—and it was big—so we knew what we could expect. When we met with the promoter, he gave us the guarantee, but he didn't give us anywhere near the amount it should have been given the number of people at the arena. We told him he owed us more money.

Completely undaunted by us he said with utter confidence and a deep Southern drawl, "No sirree. You either take what I'm giving you or I'm putting Roy back on. You saw what happened out there. He's the one they want to hear. Just take your fucking money and go."

This had never happened to us before, and we were thrown. But only for a minute, because as soon as Rick and I looked at one another we knew he was right: those kids wanted Roy to come back out and play, not the Dave Clark Five. So, as he said, we took our money and shut up about it.

Despite all the fun I was now having, by the time the tour ended I had grown to understand some things about myself. I realized from visiting my friends on the tour that I had no regrets about not being a college student. I knew I was not destined to become a dentist or a lawyer or a businessman as some of my friends were either contemplating or setting out to become. Though I wasn't entirely certain what to do, I'd seen and experienced enough about the music industry to know that while I loved every minute of it, it wasn't for me. Even though I was only nineteen years old, by the end of our tour I was exhausted, and since it was a few days before Christmas, I decided to fly home instead of returning to London. Over the holiday I did a lot of thinking about my future. I thought about how I'd grown up on my dad's movie sets and how I'd volunteered to work with every craft through the years. I knew how movies were made inside and out, and I felt at home there. I'd had a lot of fun making my high school films, and I felt confident that my early experiences had taught me a lot about how to make a movie. But the thread that runs through all of this is the fact that I always loved watching films. I am a movie fan first and foremost. What better way to spend your life than working to create the magic that allows people, myself included, to sit in a theater and be swept away?

By the end of the Christmas holiday, I knew exactly what I wanted to do: I wanted to be in the motion picture business just like my dad. So, I decided not to return to London and instead to try and start my professional life in film.

Around that same time, my sister and Ben also headed back to Los Angeles. Like me, Melinda couldn't have been happier to be coming home, with not only her three-year-old daughter, Wendy, but her new baby, Carol Ann, in tow.

8

Having made my decision, I rented a month-to-month furnished apartment and officially began my professional life.

In the spring of 1965, I earned my first real paycheck as an assistant to the producer Carroll Case. I worked on two of his movies. They were filmed back-to-back, each one in a remarkably swift five days. I was used to this kind of schedule because in the '50s, my dad would make films that quickly. I remember him shooting two films back-to-back in Kanab, Utah; one took fifteen days and the other took five. That way they could combine crew, establishing shots, etc., and save a lot of dough.

My two movies with Carroll Case fizzled in just as many days as it took to make them, but their titles deserve to live on forever: *Billy the Kid Versus Dracula,* and *Jessie James Meets Frankenstein's Daughter.* The first two films of my professional career may have disappeared long ago, but I learned that if you enjoy what you're doing—and boy did I—it didn't matter at all.

I decided to ask my father, still head of Paramount Pictures at that point, if there was a movie I could work on. Since personal conversations between us were rare and made us both uncomfortable, I kept it brief. And so did he.

I stood in front of his office desk, and said, "Hey, Dad, I'd really like a job on another movie. Can you help me?"

"Let me see what I can do," he said, and then the phone rang, which I took as my cue to leave.

It was literally that quick. But despite the brevity of our conversation (if you can call it a conversation), I knew my dad would come through for me. I always knew he wanted to help me. It does not escape me that most people who want a job working in the movies don't generally get to walk into the office of the head of a studio and ask for one. On the other hand, the fact that my father and I couldn't sustain a conversation longer than two sentences total—one for him and one for me—is an example of the confounding mix of privilege and discomfort we felt around each other.

Dad had given Sydney Pollack his first feature directing job on a movie called *The Slender Thread,* and now Sydney was ready to direct his second film. The new project was based on a Tennessee Williams one-act play called *This Property Is Condemned* and would be produced by Ray Stark for Seven Arts. For decades, Ray was one of the most powerful men in Hollywood. The movie would star Natalie Wood (be still my heart) and a young actor named Robert Redford.

Sydney went on to become one of the great directors in Hollywood, as well as a winner of two Academy Awards for producing and directing *Out of Africa.* He also made some other classic films, including *The Way We Were, Three Days of the Condor, Jeremiah Johnson, Tootsie,* and *They Shoot Horses, Don't They?*

The movie was going to shoot on stages in Los Angeles, in New Orleans, and in a small town called Bay St. Louis in Mississippi.

Shortly after I asked my dad for help, I was hired to be the assistant to production manager Clarence Eurist, who it didn't take long for me to learn had hoped *his* son would get the job. I could tell from the get-go that Clarence wasn't happy with me. The first thing he did—probably to get me out of his hair—was to send me down to Mississippi, while he stayed in LA to prep that portion of the movie.

Clarence was in his fifties and wasn't the most attractive man because he wore very thick glasses. Only one of his eyes focused straight ahead, while the other wandered. He was stern and impersonal with me, talking like a boss might speak to his least favorite employee, the one he really hopes will fail so he can fire his ass ASAP.

"You're flying down with our production designer Stephen Grimes to handle all the preproduction issues in Mississippi until we get there."

"Okay" was all I felt safe enough to say, even though I wondered if there'd be anyone there to help me. At nineteen that was a very big responsibility and could have been a setup for failure. But it turns out I did have help.

I arrived in Mississippi with Stephen, who later won an Oscar for *Out of Africa,* just like Sydney did. He became my mentor and champion whenever I needed it.

I was to organize everything for the filming in Mississippi, things like getting city permits, dealing with local schools and police, signing location agreements (in the 1960s there was no such thing as a location manager), and even organizing extras to work as background.

Even though this was my first big movie, I was comfortable doing the work. I had an instinctual ability, having grown up on movie sets, and my work in London organizing, budgeting, and dealing with talent taught me a lot. Despite that nascent professional confidence, however, none of my previous experience prepared me for what I was about to learn about the world and the pervasive bigotry of the deep South.

The Civil Rights Movement had the goal of securing the same legal rights for African Americans that every other American already had. The movement sought to bring an end to segregation, exploitation, discrimination, and violence against African Americans. It's just that the fervent desire to enact these changes was met with an equally vehement push against it.

By the time I—a privileged white kid—arrived in Bay, St. Louis in 1965, I had the luxury of naively assuming that attitudes had changed.

I went to meet the principal of the elementary school to find student extras for our film. I told him a bit about the movie and explained that once we acquired parental permission, we would need the names, addresses, and phone numbers of their kids. Once the wardrobe people got there, we'd measure the kids and fit them for their clothes so when we needed them to work, they'd already be "wardrobe ready" when we called them in.

The principal squinted at me through his big bushy eyebrows and said, "Mr. Koch, none of our little white kids are gonna play with no n******, are they?"

I felt as if he'd slapped me in the face. I was also disgusted but knew better than to let that show. And I was frightened, because I knew at that moment that this man was articulating a sentiment that was still alive and thriving in the South. With as little emotion as possible, I said, "Well, no, this movie takes place in 1931, so the white and black kids won't be playing together."

He said, "Well, that's good."

I thought we were done but the man had more venom to spew. The mystery of why he was staring at the top of my head revealed itself when he said, "Say, Mr. Koch, are you a Jew?"

Trying to retain my composure, and thereby not reveal exactly how scared I was, l said, "Yes, I am."

"You know I ain't never seen a Jew before—up close."

He was looking for horns.

I've thought about this man many times. He became the symbol of a kind of hatred I didn't know existed. This man, whom I am confident infused the children he taught with the same racism, catapulted me outside the boundary of my own ignorance. I knew from the moment I left his presence that I would never be the same.

★ ★ ★

We were two weeks away from shooting when Sydney Pollack, Ray Stark, Clarence Eurist, cinematographer James Wong Howe, and producer John Houseman finally came to town.

It was an extremely exciting time. I stood in the back of the group as they walked the sets. I got to be there listening, and I was in awe. I had worked on these two shitty little movies before, and now here I was in the presence of all these legends. John Houseman would go on to star in *The Paper Chase* but was already famous for working with Orson Welles on *Citizen Kane.* And James Wong Howe won Oscars for both *The Rose Tattoo* and *Hud,* one of my all-time favorites, and here I was working with him!

I was following them silently, pinching myself, when Sydney turned to Clarence and said, "I want to shoot over here. Can I shoot this way, Clarence?"

Clarence—who really didn't know because he'd just arrived—stumbled and said hesitatingly, "Uh, I think so."

I blurted out with uncensored and naïve enthusiasm, "Oh yeah, that's Mrs. so-and-so's place, and I have the location agreements right here!"

Everybody turned and looked at me. That was the moment I realized I should have kept my mouth shut, or quietly told Clarence, my boss, that yes, the location was available, and then he could relay the good news to Sydney. But I was a nineteen-year-old assistant, and I still had a thing or two to learn about politics and tact.

Clarence was an excellent production manager who knew his job backward and forward. He was never a fan of mine, and I don't think my jumping in like that endeared me to him. Even so, I think they all—possibly even Clarence—couldn't help but see that I had done my job. At least that's what I told myself.

The first day of shooting was thrilling, and I was running back and forth loving every minute of whatever job I was given. We were filming on a railroad trestle, which required the first assistant director (AD), a man in his sixties with a bad ankle, to walk up and down that trestle. By ten o'clock that morning, the first AD had quit, realizing his ankle wasn't strong enough to carry him all day. Since the second assistant director had to step in right away, someone needed to do *that* job. They threw me in to do it.

Let me clarify the responsibilities of a first AD. Prior to shooting a film, the first AD does a script breakdown, a detailed analysis of every dramatic action in the film and what will be required to create it. The breakdown is used to finalize the budget and prepare the film for production.

The first AD is the director's right—and most of the time left—arm. They work together to prepare the movie for production, down to the last detail. Once production is underway, the first AD is directly responsible to the director and runs the floor, or set.

When everything's ready for the scene to be shot, the first AD calls, "Rolling" and the director calls, "Action." What happens next is like the moment in baseball when the pitcher throws the ball toward home plate. Every person—player, fan, and peanut seller—is expending every ounce of themselves, their full and focused attention, on that play. The attention of the moviemaking team is similarly focused on getting the shot. For me, there's simply nothing better than being a part of that team.

The second AD functions as the first AD's right hand. The second is the one who writes up the call sheets, brings the actors to the floor when they're supposed to be there, and sets the background action with the first AD.

Whatever career you choose, it helps to know your strong suit. As I look back, organizing a film shoot was mine. I cut my teeth in the '60s and early '70s when there was only a first and a second. It boggles my mind to think of the scenes we pulled off on the streets of New York City, with two of the biggest celebrities in the world, Barbra Streisand and Robert Redford, making *The Way We Were*. It was just me as the first AD and Jerry Ziesmer as my second, but between the two of us, we managed to get it all done on schedule. To do those same scenes today, would require a first, a second, a second second, a third, twelve assistants, and twenty cops. I know, I know, times have changed.

Here I was on *This Property Is Condemned* having been moved up to second AD. After the first week of filming, neither Sydney nor John Houseman, the producer, were happy with the work of the guy who had been promoted to first. They brought down a new, more experienced first and expected the guy who'd been promoted to move back to his original job as the second AD. That guy decided he didn't want to be a second anymore, so he quit. Now they had a brand-new first and no second. Since I was the only one with continuity on the film, and they liked the job I had been doing when I was thrown in as the second, they asked me to stay on in that role and got a waiver from the Directors Guild of America to let me continue to work in that capacity.

While the new first was quite qualified and good at his job, sometimes he liked to take a nip or two at lunch, which rendered him just inebriated enough to be incapable of work by the time the afternoon rolled around.

Before I knew what was happening, they handed me a bullhorn, a whistle, a huge walkie-talkie and said, "This afternoon, you're running the set." I had watched first ADs for fifteen years but actually doing it was a lot harder. The first day or two I was blowing into the walkie-talkie and talking into the whistle, but eventually I got the hang of it and loved every minute. I played team sports my whole childhood, but being an integral part of a movie family made me feel like I truly belonged.

One might have talent, one might be good at their job, but I do believe that luck has an awful lot to do with how you move forward in life. And boy, was I lucky! If all those circumstances hadn't happened, I might never have had the opportunity.

One of the jobs of the second AD is to let the actors know when they're needed on the set. The first day Natalie Wood was to work, it was my job to inform her when to come to set. I bolted across a vast dirt expanse to her trailer. I knocked on her door, but it stayed closed as she said sweetly through it, "I'll be out in a few minutes."

I—in my naïveté—said, "Oh, but we're ready now. Mr. Howe said the light is perfect."

The door opened, she looked at me with those big brown eyes of hers, and said, "Oh, okay," as she stepped down the metal steps of the trailer.

Natalie Wood was my favorite actress, and I had a crush on her mainly from *Splendor in the Grass,* but also from *Gypsy, West Side Story,* and *Love with the Proper Stranger.*

She took my arm—and my breath away—not only because I loved her, but because as soon as the trailer door opened, I was overwhelmed with the scent of an oversprayed perfume, which I would later learn was called Jungle Gardenia. Natalie was doused in the stuff.

I walked her, my queen, to the set, feeling like a king dangerously close to asphyxiation.

Later, everyone asked me how I managed to get her there since she was often late.

"I don't know. I just told her the truth—that our DP said the light was perfect."

Two of the many lessons I've learned in this business, I learned that day: The truth is reliable, so make sure you tell it. And actors and actresses want to look their best, so mentioning to Natalie, one of the most beautiful women in the world, that the light was right turned out to be the perfect motivation for her to leave the safety of her trailer on time and be ready to perform.

The schedule for *This Property Is Condemned* started with us shooting in Mississippi, then going to Los Angeles for stage work, and finally on to New Orleans for the final portion of the shoot. I was asked to accompany Natalie on her flight from Los Angeles to New Orleans to make sure everything went smoothly for our star. Gulp. The thought of just me and Natalie alone on a plane together made me shiver.

By the time we were headed to New Orleans, Natalie trusted me to take care of everything for her. I knew how to protect her from people wanting access to her. I knew how to get her in and out of public spaces quickly and easily.

Once on the plane, we settled in for the three-and-a-half-hour flight and shared a conversation about the film and everything else that was going on in the world. We talked about desegregation, the Civil Rights Act, and the ongoing war in Vietnam. And we gossiped.

When the captain instructed us to be sure our seat belts were fastened, as we were about to land, I was disappointed that my intimate time with Natalie was about to come to an end. Just as the landing gear went down, and seconds before we hit the runway, the plane shot straight up in the air with such a powerful thrust that every single passenger gasped in shock. Natalie grabbed my arm. We looked in each other's eyes, sharing a moment of terror and wondering if we were about to die. At the speed of light, I went from that concern to a thought that only a nineteen-year-old might have: if I'm going to die, I'm going to kiss Natalie Wood before I do.

At the exact moment I started to move toward her, the captain came on the intercom and announced that everything was fine. He explained that the reason he pulled the plane up so suddenly was that just when we were about to touch down, another plane had come onto our runway. The good news was we landed safely. The bad news was I never did get to kiss Natalie Wood.

★ ★ ★

Even though I never kissed her, I was incredibly fortunate to work with Natalie and so many other great talents on *This Property Is Condemned.*

I really wanted to learn as much as I could from our cinematographer, James Wong Howe. One day we were shooting on the top of that railroad trestle with two young actors, Mary Badham, who played Scout in *To Kill a Mockingbird*, and John Provost, who played Timmy in the *Lassie* television and movie productions. They were both in their early teens.

It was a beautiful day, bald blue sky, but around three thirty or four in the afternoon, Mr. Howe said, "The light's no good. We have to wrap." So we wrapped. I didn't understand the decision since it was a gorgeous day, but I kept my mouth shut, as I noticed everyone else did. I concluded that since this was the revered James Wong Howe, no one was going to question him.

We were on the same trestle the next day, with the same two young actors and another bald blue sky. That afternoon around three thirty or four I waited to hear Mr. Howe say the light was no good again, but he didn't. Five o'clock came and went, as did six. Finally, at a quarter till seven, the great man announced, "I'm out of light. We have to wrap."

One of my jobs was to see that the crew got into cars that would take them back to the hotel. As I was putting Mr. Howe in his car, I got up the nerve to speak to him: "Mr. Howe, I'm trying to learn, so is it okay if I ask you a question?"

"Sure, it is."

"How come yesterday we lost the light around three thirty and yet today with the same weather conditions, we were able to work till six forty-five?"

He looked at me and with a slight wink and said, "Yesterday I had a golf game."

★ ★ ★

The most important experience I had on that movie was one that informed my work ethic for the rest of my career. I was in the bathroom close to the set when a couple of crew guys walked in. I couldn't see them from my stall, but I could hear them.

"Hey, you know that kid Howard Koch, Jr.?" one of them said. "He only got the job because his father is head of Paramount."

My heart sank because the first thing that came to mind was, that is why I'm here. It has nothing to do with who I am or what I can do. It's because of who my father is.

I wanted to dig a hole and crawl into it. I had wondered at times how I could go into the same business as my father, carrying the same name as him, and *not* expect people to compare us. In those moments, I would tell myself I was going to have to learn to deal with it since the movie business is what I knew and what I loved. But at this moment, overhearing what a fellow crew member said about me, it crushed me.

The other guy answered, "Yeah, that's true. That is how he got here, but he's doing a good job, and he's a good kid too, so why don't you give him a break?"

Because the man delivered his response without an ounce of judgment, I heard it without any defenses rushing in to protect me. In that moment, delivered by his kindness, I caught a glimpse of the depth of my own confusion, as each of these questions surfaced: What was it going to take for me to become my own man in this business? How will I ever find a way to make a name for myself, to be seen independent of my father, when I share his name, and that's all anyone ever seems to notice?

9

While I was working on *Property*, the Vietnam War was really heating up, and there wasn't a kid my age, myself included, who wasn't worried about being called upon to serve. I got my notice from Selective Service in September 1965, summoning me to appear in downtown LA, and believe me, I was scared shitless. Not only that, I didn't want to go fight a war I vehemently opposed.

My conviction deepened when Mr. Peterson, one of my favorite high school teachers, lost his son Denny in Vietnam. When my friends and I heard Denny had been killed, we went over to pay our respects to his dad. I don't know what we said, but I remember that Mr. Peterson was crying. I'd never seen a man that close to his feelings before and his palpable pain hit me hard. I did not want to be a soldier, much less part of that war.

I was desperate to find a way to get out of the draft, knowing that neither a move to Canada, which some guys I knew had made, nor a college deferment would work for me.

I made my plans to fly home from our filming location for my appointment, but in the meantime, I called two of my doctors to ask if they'd write letters on my behalf. Dr. Cline, the orthopedist who'd operated twice on my broken leg, wrote a textbook-length treatise about how my weak ankle would prevent me from being stable enough to reliably serve my country and help my fellow soldiers. The other doctor, Dr. Hoytt, who'd been my general practitioner and had been taking care of me most of my life, wrote one (what I thought of as lame) sentence: "Howard has had intermittent allergies throughout his life and severe bronchial asthma on occasion."

Thanks a lot, Doc, for all your trouble.

Even though what he said was true, I was pissed at the little effort he had exerted on my behalf, and I was certain that if I were to rely on his letter alone, boot camp and a buzz cut would be looming in my not too distant future.

I showed up for my appointment, had my physical, and, while standing in my underwear, was allowed to show the physician my letters. Of course, I began with the tome from Dr. Cline, but after reading the first few sentences about my weak ankle, he glanced up and threw a look at me that felt like he'd just lobbed a live grenade and tossed the letter in the trash. With zero confidence I handed him the one-liner my lazy GP had written.

He read it, took one look back at me, and said, "You're out."

"What?" I asked incredulously.

"I said you're out. You're 1Y."

I only knew that 4F meant the army would never take you, so that's the number/letter combo that I was aiming for. I didn't have a clue what 1Y meant.

"What's that?" I asked.

The guy—100 percent stoic military man speaking without inflection—said, "That means when they start taking women and children, they'll take you too. But not before. Next in line."

He might not have felt any emotion, but I sure as hell did. My whole body released. I still wanted to be 4F though, and I still had a couple of other examinations with different doctors to get through before I could really relax.

When it came to the next part of the exam, where they check your heart and then put the stethoscope on your back to listen to your chest, I took full advantage of the three packs of cigarettes I had continuously smoked the night before, and I wheezed with as much of a rasp as I could when the next doctor said, "Breathe."

"What's that?" he asked sounding a bit concerned.

"What's what?"

"Breathe again." I wheezed again.

When he heard my breathing he looked down on my chart—we all had charts—and then he confirmed. "Oh, you have asthma."

"Yes, does that make me 4F?" I asked a little too hopefully.

"No, no, you're 1Y," he answered kindly, as if he—unlike the automaton before him—actually did have blood running through his veins.

It turns out to be true that the things from which we suffer can actually deliver hidden gifts, boons. Thanks to asthma, I did not go to Vietnam.

★ ★ ★

During *Property*, which I could now return to without the shadow of being drafted looming over me, Redford and I had become friends. We had a mutual love of movies, and we always had something to share with one another about sports. On Sundays, we'd play golf together, and from time to time we'd toss a football.

Bob was not only great looking but a terrific actor to boot. Though he wasn't a movie star yet, everyone knew he was on a fast track to stardom, but this was before *Butch Cassidy and the Sundance Kid*.

One day while we were filming in Los Angeles, he said to me, "I've got this house and some land in Utah and I want to drive up there this weekend. Why don't you come? We'll trade off driving all night so we can get there Saturday morning. We'll hang out and then drive back late Sunday in time to be on set by Monday morning."

That sounded like a great plan, so I said, "Sure, why not?"

Bob drove a Lincoln Continental in those days. We left Paramount around seven o'clock Friday night and drove all the way to Vegas, sharing the driving and stopping at an all-you-can-eat dive along the way.

We'd been talking and talking all the while we drove. We talked about the movie, about sports, and about the A-frame house Bob and his wife, Lola, had built—casual conversation that any two guy friends driving through the desert would be having.

I had been driving for about two hours since leaving Vegas when all of a sudden in the middle of God-only-knows what pitch-black desert in Nevada, Bob said, "Pull off the road."

"Why Bob?" I asked.

The idea unnerved me but he insisted. "Just pull off, just pull over. Trust me."

His voice was authoritative, insistent, so I pulled off the main road onto a side road and kept driving until he said, "Pull over there."

"There? That's dirt," I said, stating the obvious but trying to hide my growing fear.

"Just pull over and stop."

In nearly the same instant as I pulled over and put the brake on, Bob shoved the gear shift into park, turned off the engine, grabbed the keys, and said harshly, "Get out."

If this were a scene in a movie, it would be the moment where the friend of the handsome, popular guy realizes his pal is a serial killer and he's about to have his throat cut. As close as I felt Bob and I were, it occurred to me at the moment he insisted I get out of the car that, in fact, I barely knew him. My heart was thundering right out of my chest as I got out of the car, making sure to stay on my side of the Lincoln's vast hood.

I tried to clock the expression on his face. *Is that a scowl? I think that's a scowl.* I scanned his pockets for bulges that might reveal the presence of a hidden gun or knife. Braver men than I might have run or fought, but instead, just as I began to feel my legs about to buckle underneath me in sheer terror, Bob began to scream, a long, let-it-all-out scream that clearly had nothing to do with me.

When it was over, he looked at me satisfied, smiled, threw me the keys, and said, "Try it. It'll be good for you."

Still shaken and not understanding why he wanted me to, I tried to scream, but only a pitiful little "Ehhhh" sound eked its way up from my totally constricted throat and squeaked out of my mouth.

Even though I was squeaking, all the tension I felt was gone, and I realized that it had been one of Bob's practical jokes all along. Man, did he get me!

We got back in the car, and as we headed up to Utah, he told me all about Arthur Janov's primal scream therapy and how it was supposed to release suppressed trauma.

We stayed that weekend in Redford's A-frame house on the land that would later become Sundance. With everything Sundance has become since then, whenever it comes across my radar, I still can't help but remember the night Bob Redford almost slit my throat.

10

By the time I finished *Property*, word had gotten out that I was good at my job, which I'd hoped was the sole reason that William Castle, who had been a B-horror movie producer/director, offered me a job in early 1966.

Of course, the fact that Bill had a deal at Paramount to make horror films for my dad likely also played a role. I could never be sure, but whatever the reason or reasons, I became Bill's assistant, making $110 a week. I read scripts. I made budgets. I did whatever was needed.

Bill didn't drive, so one of my jobs was to pick him up in the morning and get him to his office at the studio.

The mornings were cold, and Bill wanted the windows up, which would have been fine with me except that without fail, he'd light up a cigar the length of my thigh and smoke us both out. I was usually green by the time we arrived at the studio.

He was a larger-than-life showman filled with amazingly entertaining stories. One of my favorites concerned the time he was a young guy working for Orson Welles at the Mercury Theatre in New York when Welles went on the radio and said aliens were attacking as part of *The War of the Worlds* broadcast. It caused a mass panic. (The "other" Howard Koch was the guy who actually adapted H. G. Welles's story for Orson.)

When the nationwide hysteria had passed, Bill told Orson, "What I really want to do is go out to Hollywood and make movies."

Orson helped him out and one day told him, "I got you a meeting with Harry Cohn, the head of Columbia Pictures. It's up to you now, but I wrote Harry a letter and told him you were a good guy. I said he should give you a job."

Bill was beside himself with gratitude and made the move to California not knowing a soul. As he tells it, the night before his meeting, he went to Columbia, at the corner of Sunset and Gower, just to walk around the outside of the studio. He certainly couldn't get in until his meeting the next day.

Bill saw a bar across the street and walked in to have a drink, feeling excited about his meeting, even a little full of himself. He sat at one end of the bar, which was empty except for one man at the opposite end. He was feeling chipper and fun because he's young and because he's about to meet the head of Columbia Pictures.

He said to the guy at the other end of the bar, "Hey, let me buy you a drink."

The guy refused politely with a simple, "No, that's okay."

Bill kept at him, refusing to accept the man's obvious desire to be left alone. "No, I'd really like to buy you a drink."

"No thanks" was all the guy said back.

Bill finished his drink; the guy was still sipping his. A few minutes later Bill ordered another drink and, loosened up a bit now, walked over to the man. "C'mon, let me buy you a drink. I'm William Castle, and I know Harry Cohn personally."

Of course, he hadn't met Harry Cohn yet, but the other guy must have found his chutzpah amusing, so he said, "Hi, Bill, I'm George Stevens," who just happened to be one of the most famous directors in Hollywood.

Bill, ashamed, tripped all over himself saying, "Oh, Mr. Stevens, I'm so sorry. I didn't know it was you. I'm out here from New York, and I really don't know Harry Cohn, but I'm going to meet him tomorrow. Gee, just to meet you is such a privilege."

Mr. Stevens said kindly, "Oh, it's all right. What are you here to do?"

"Well, I'm looking for a job because I want to work in the movies."

They talked a bit, Bill shared his experience with Orson Welles, and eventually George said, "Well, Bill, when you see Harry tomorrow, tell him you can be my dialogue director on my new film."

Bill couldn't believe his good fortune. "Oh, Mr. Stevens, thank you so much, sir."

The next day, he went to meet Harry Cohn, who was right up there in the Hollywood stratosphere with Louis B. Mayer, Darryl Zanuck, and Jack Warner. Bill was nervous, talking too much and too fast.

"Mr. Cohn, it's so nice to meet you, thank you for seeing me. I worked for Orson Welles, and that made me want to be in the movies, so I'm here now hoping to get a job."

Mr. Cohn said, "Yeah, I received Orson's letter but tell me, what do you want to do?"

Bill was delighted to be able to say, "Well, I met George Stevens last night, and he said I could be the dialogue director on his next movie for you."

Mr. Cohn said, "Well, Bill, if George said that, then you've got the job."

The movie was *Penny Serenade,* starring Cary Grant and Irene Dunne. Bill assumed—as anyone who didn't know any better might—that the dialogue director directed the dialogue. The first day of shooting was a scene between the two stars, and Bill was holding the script while standing near the camera. George Stevens yelled, "Action," and right off the bat, Cary Grant flubbed the line.

The minute Bill Castle heard that he yelled, "Cut! Cary, you read the line wrong."

Silence. You could have heard a pin drop if anyone had been stupid enough to drop one at that moment. George Stevens turned around to face Bill Castle and reached for him like he was going to choke him or punch him or something similarly regrettable.

Cary Grant came to the rescue by saying, "Wait a minute! Wait a minute, George. Bill's right. I read the line wrong. Let's do it once more."

That interruption was just enough time for George Stevens to collect himself, calm down, and say to Bill, "If you ever open your mouth again on my set, I *will* kill you."

Bill, scared out of his mind, never made a mistake like that again.

During the course of the movie, he and Cary Grant became friends. Since Bill didn't drive, Cary offered to pick him up at the bus stop right in front of Schwab's Pharmacy on Sunset Boulevard so they could drive in together.

One day, as Bill told it, there were two beautiful girls waiting at the bus stop when he arrived on foot. Being friendly and a bit flirty he said, "Good morning, ladies. How are you doing this morning?"

They said something that didn't really extend the conversation, so Bill, persisting, said, "Are you waiting for the bus?"

Looking at him as if he was an idiot, they said, "Of course we're waiting for the bus! It's a bus stop. Aren't you?"

"No, I'm not. I'm waiting for Cary Grant to pick me up."

Now they'd had it with him. "Of course, you are," they said, turning away and ending the conversation right there.

But just at that moment, up pulled Cary Grant in his Rolls-Royce convertible.

"Morning, Bill!" he said cheerily, whereupon Bill jumped in the car and waved good-bye to the girls, who he insisted were still sitting at that bus stop, frozen in time.

★　★　★

One weekend while I was working for Bill, I was shopping when I ran into Rita Litter. Although we'd lost touch, we'd known each other since the fifth grade. She was one of my grade school dance partners. Back then I liked her right away. By seventh grade, we were attending most of the school dances together. I'll never forget one memorable night with Rita. We were slow dancing, probably to something romantic like Johnny Mathis's "Chances Are." Our bodies were pressed so close to one another that it brought up—well—things I'd never felt before. It was such a new and delicious sensation that I told my besotted self, *Wow! I think I want to marry her!*

I was happy to see her after so many years. Standing together on the street and not wanting the moment to end, I said, "Hey, I've got two tickets to tonight's premiere of *A Man for All Seasons*. Do you want to join me?"

Rita, who tended toward the sarcastic, said, "Sure, why not? I've got nothing better to do."

That date led to many more, and before long, we'd fallen in love.

I always wanted what my parents had: a partner with whom I would share an abiding love. Although I wasn't aware of it at the time, I suppose my other expectation was that my wife would worship me just as my mother did my father.

Everything about Rita was familiar and comfortable to me—we were in carpool together from the time we were twelve years old, and she fit the picture I had in mind for my married-forever-just-like-my-parents scenario. It wasn't long before I realized that my declaration while dancing with Rita all those years ago was still true: I really did want to marry her. When Rita and I reconnected and fell in love, we were sure we'd found our foreverness in one another.

Shortly after I started working for Bill, Redford signed on to make *Barefoot in the Park*. It was a nice compliment to me that Bob went to producer Hal Wallis and director Gene Saks to request that I be the dialogue coach on the film. Years earlier, the Directors Guild had become a reputable force in the movie industry, and the members objected to the word "director" being used by the person fact-checking the dialogue. From that day forward, that person became known as the dialogue coach.

Bill allowed me to stop working for him during this period of time so I could take the job.

* * *

While working on *Barefoot*, I was back in LA when Bob loaned me his house in Benedict Canyon so that I'd have a nice romantic place to take Rita, since I intended to ask her to marry me. We had a great dinner, I gave her the ring, and just like that we were on our way to following in the familiar footprint of our parents' lives.

* * *

After *Barefoot,* I went back to working for Bill again. I came into his office very early one morning and started to read a manuscript. I'm a slow reader so a book that size would normally have taken me days to finish, but it was so gripping, I was done in three hours. I thought it was the greatest thing I'd ever read, so much so that when Bill came in, I said, "You gotta buy the rights to this right away."

Bill got on a plane and headed for New York. By the next morning, when everyone else had read it, Bill was on a plane headed back to Los Angeles, having already purchased the rights to *Rosemary's Baby* for $100,000.

The tenure of the head of a studio varies greatly. In 1966 when Paramount Pictures was bought by Charles Bludhorn's Gulf & Western Industries, my father was fired and was replaced by Robert Evans. Ours is a town where prestigious titles matter. When you have one, you're hot; if you lose it, you're suddenly cold as ice. As evidence of this fact, during the Christmas seasons when my father was head of Paramount, the staggering number of gifts that showed up at their house on Crescent Drive filled their family room. I remember one particular basket from John Wayne that literally went from floor to ceiling. When my dad was no longer head of the studio, our family room was empty, but the message was overflowing with meaning.

Bill was about to get a pretty strong message of his own with regard to *Rosemary's Baby*. I was in the office working that morning when Robert Evans called and said, "Bill's gotta come back into the studio and see me as soon as he lands."

When Bill got back, he went to see Evans. Bill emerged from that meeting a bit stunned, having sold the rights he'd only just purchased to Paramount, for $250,000. It's true he made a lot of money in a very short time on the deal, but he'd also signed a contract to produce the movie that included a clause giving him only "best efforts to direct." Evans thought Roman Polanski was the perfect director, so unfortunately, Bill ended up losing his chance to direct, a defeat from which he never recovered.

11

While Polanski was writing the screenplay for *Rosemary's Baby*, we were in a holding pattern. I was surprised and excited to be asked by Gene Saks to be the dialogue coach on my dad's film *The Odd Couple*. I had been Gene's dialogue coach the year before on *Barefoot*.

As is usually the case after being fired, former studio heads tend to transition to on-the-lot producer positions. This was true for my father, and part of his severance was to be able to produce the Neil Simon play, which he had bought when he was still in charge.

Sinatra wanted to star in it along with Jackie Gleason, and my father felt a mix of pressure from and loyalty to Frank to put that package together. However, Walter Matthau, who had starred in *The Odd Couple* on Broadway, paid my father a visit. Walter, who at the time was a well-known actor but not a star, looked Dad in the eye and said, "Do you really want Neil Simon's best play ever to be a movie with Frank Sinatra and Jackie Gleason? I don't think so." He went on to say, "I should play Oscar, and the only person who should play Felix is Jack Lemmon. Howard, you know I'm right." My dad knew he was, and so the rest is history, but the relationship between Frank and my dad cooled for many years after that.

This would be the first time I'd work with my father. Growing up I had watched my dad work many times, but now that I was a professional and no longer a kid volunteering on his set, I was nervous.

I was actually going to be working with him in a real job. I got to see firsthand why everyone was so enamored with him as a producer. He made everyone on the film feel like they were important, while at the same time, he made sure the movie stayed on track. I was impressed with him too and wanted to show him what I could do.

Working on *The Odd Couple* allowed me to work with two of my favorite actors, Jack Lemmon as the fastidious Felix Unger, and Walter Matthau as Oscar Madison, the slob. While I was the dialogue coach, I was also unofficially being mentored as an assistant director by the first AD, Hank Moonjean.

Walter was definitely one of a kind. One day we were shooting a scene with Herb Edelman, as Murray the cop, and Walter in a police car on Broadway on the Upper West Side in New York. We had an insert car hooked up to the police car. (An insert car is basically a truck that is attached to the car being filmed. The vehicle is outfitted with lights, cameras, and any other necessary equipment.)

There were a lot of lights on the insert car in order to get good light on Walter and Herb. I was lying in the back seat with the director, Gene Saks, both of us trying to stay out of sight. It must have been a hundred degrees outside. We had to keep the windows up and couldn't have the air conditioning on in order to keep noise to a minimum so the sound could be recorded perfectly. We were dying back there, but Walter kept blowing the lines—not intentionally of course; it just happened. And for each line he blew, we had to go all the way around the block and come back again to set up for another take. It was taxing, and it was taking forever, but finally on take six or so, Walter was doing great, and the scene was going to be over soon. However, just as he was about to finish, he interrupted himself and said, "Hey, wait a minute! Wait a minute!" and then we heard the window rolling down.

Gene and I were looking at each other from our scrunched-up positions on the seat, wondering what the hell was going on.

Suddenly we heard Walter yelling out the window, "Hey, Mom! Mom! It's me, Wally. I'm in a movie here!" His mom just happened to be walking down upper Broadway when Walter spotted her!

The magnificent Jack Lemmon was the consummate professional. As much as he would laugh and kid and look like he wasn't paying attention prior to a take or a scene, when the AD called, "Roll camera," Jack would immediately and fully transform himself into his character by saying aloud, as if conjuring the healing powers of his own personal incantation, "Magic time."

I believe the custom started when Jack played a flawed character named Joe Clay in the 1962 movie *Days of Wine and Roses*. In uttering those two words, "Magic time," Clay, an alcoholic, casts a personal spell before he takes a much-needed sip of booze. Whether or not Jack ad-libbed the line, it was so powerful and transformative a phrase for him that he appropriated it and used it as the vehicle for getting into all the different characters he played.

I've repeated Jack's mantra to many actors over the years, but the person it had the most profound effect on was me. I've used it to focus myself every time we're about to shoot a scene, or before I have to make a speech, but my connection to it goes deeper than that. It transports me all the way back to when I visited my dad on a movie set for the very first time. That's when I was transformed from a scared little kid to a delighted boy transfixed by everything he saw unfolding. That was the day I learned that, for me, movies—both making them and watching them—are and always will be my personal magic time.

One of the more complicated issues involved in shooting *The Odd Couple* was a scene we wanted to film at Shea Stadium. Walter's character is a sportswriter who is covering a game between the Mets and the Pirates. We had to get permission from Major League Baseball, the New York Mets, *and* the Pittsburgh Pirates to film them at the stadium. There were contracts and all sorts of legal hurdles to scale.

We presented the scene to the higher-ups at those organizations, and naturally were met with "What are *we* going to get out of it?"

Great producer that he was, my dad came up with an idea. "How about we make it 'Odd Couple Day' at Shea Stadium? We'll have Walter and Jack there to sign autographs, and you can interview them. They'll do whatever you want. You can promote the hell out of it and get a much bigger afternoon game attendance. That's what's in it for you."

They agreed, so we moved on to the next challenge.

The game was to start at two o'clock, which would mean we would have from one thirty to one fifty, to shoot our scene. A mere twenty minutes.

Walter and Heywood Hale Broun, a famous sports writer, were to be sitting in the press box watching the game when Heywood would announce, "Well, the Mets are up one-nothing, top of the ninth, no outs, bases loaded, Clemente up. The Mets are gonna lose another one."

After Broun said his line, Matthau would say, with a mouthful of hotdog, "What's the matter? You never heard of a triple play?"

Just as he says that the phone rings and somebody yells, "Hey, Oscar, it's for you."

Oscar turns away from the game, still chewing, and picks up the phone. It's Felix, who says, "Oscar, don't eat any dogs at the game today 'cause I'm making franks 'n beans for dinner."

As Felix is saying that, a triple play happens, and since there was no such thing as instant replay back then, Oscar—who had his back to the field to answer the phone—misses the play. Oscar proceeds to go insane because he missed one of the rarest plays in baseball.

One of my jobs was to go down to the field and work with the Pirates, the Mets, and the umpires so that we could pull off that triple play at the appropriate time during the scene. First, I went to the Mets and explained that they'd be the team on the field. The idea was that when Clemente came up, they'd throw a pitch wherever he wanted, he'd hit into the triple play, and the Mets would go crazy and run off the field. The Mets, of course, agreed.

Then I went to the Pirates and talked to Roberto Clemente (yes, all you sports fans, I really did get to meet Roberto Clemente), their Hall of Fame right fielder and one of the greatest baseball players of all time. I told him the plan, and he said, "Okay, but I want ten thousand dollars to do it."

It was a hitch, that's for sure, but I wasn't too surprised because naturally, Clemente wouldn't like the idea of hitting into a triple play. A home run maybe, but not a triple play.

I radioed up to my dad and his response when I told him what Clemente wanted in order to hit into the triple play was, "No way we're paying ten thousand dollars. Who else ya got?"

I went back to the Pirate's dugout, and I recognized a World Series hero, second baseman Bill Mazeroski. He had hit a home run in the ninth inning of the seventh game of the 1960 World Series for the Pirates to beat the Yankees. I asked him if he'd do it.

"Sure, I'll do it for five hundred bucks."

I didn't bother to call back upstairs, I just said, "You got a deal."

We were all ready to go as it neared one thirty, but the only problem was the umpires hadn't come on the field yet. When they finally showed up, I met with them at home plate, and I explained what was about to happen.

I said, "Mazeroski's gonna hit a hard ground ball to the third baseman. He will step on the bag, throw to second, and the second baseman will throw to first to complete the triple play. When the play's over, just do what umps do at the end of a game—walk or run off the field—and each time I'll ask you to come back for another take, and we'll hit into another triple play until it works."

"Got it," they said.

So far so good.

Then I asked, "Who's the first base umpire?" Turned out it was Augie Donatelli, a short, loud Italian man. Here's how I know he was loud: I said, "Augie, if it's a close play at first, call him out because, from the angle of our cameras in the press box, we'll never be able to see whether the guy was out or safe. Then we'll get out of your hair so you can play the real game."

Augie looked at me and while shoving—hard—at my shoulder with his pointer finger, said extremely loudly, "Listen, kid. I've been callin' 'em as I see 'em for twenty-five years and I ain't gonna change that for any goddamn movie!"

After several takes, we'd gotten our play. We'd actually gotten our play a few times, but to be safe, to make sure we had it, we did extra takes until we knew we were covered. That's typical.

When it was all done, I thanked the Pirates, the Mets, and the umpires. That's when Augie Donatelli called me over and said, not so loudly, "I want you to understand something: there are thirty thousand fans in Shea Stadium today. If I called him out when he was safe, I could never umpire again at Shea for all the crap they'd give me. You gotta call 'em as you see 'em, kid."

I think that's great life advice offered by one helluva ump.

Meanwhile, Rita and I had set a date to get married at the Ambassador Hotel right after *The Odd Couple* finished filming, but her father had a sudden heart attack one week before the wedding, so of course, we canceled our plans. Fortunately, he came through it fine and in June 1967, we married in their living room with thirty family members and friends present instead of the 130 we had intended to invite to the hotel.

12

Although Bill Castle couldn't direct *Rosemary's Baby,* he was the producer, and since I was still working for him, I was both his assistant and his (now very experienced) dialogue coach.

Mia Farrow and I were the youngest people on the movie, so it made sense that we'd become friends. She was married to Frank Sinatra at the time and was a whopping twenty-nine years his junior. Flute thin, almost fragile, Mia had that short haircut that really set her apart. We had a lot of fun together.

When we finished shooting in New York, we had the Labor Day weekend off, so Mia said, "Hey, Frank's playing in Vegas and I'm stopping there on my way home. Wanna come?"

"Yeah, sure, I'll go to Vegas." I loved that idea.

Jilly Rizzo, Frank's protector and the owner of his favorite saloon in NYC, Jilly's, was there to meet us when we got off the plane. Jilly's eyes never looked at you straight. One looked one way and one looked the other. With that quirk of birth, it meant he wasn't going to miss much. He told Mia to get in the car because "Frank wants to see you."

We drove to the Sands Hotel where I was handed my keys and directed to my room, right next to Frank and Mia's enormous suite. Mia put her stuff down and then we were taken to Frank's dressing room where they saw each other for the first time in six weeks. I knew things were rocky when instead of wrapping his arms around her and planting a big wet one on her lips, he gave her a tepid peck on the cheek and sent us off to see Don Rickles's set at the Sahara. Don did a whole gag about Frank and Mia when he saw her. Mia was laughing, fully appreciating the joke. She was my age—just twenty-one—so she knew when we went to see Rickles that he'd take some potshots at her, but Mia also knew it was all in fun.

We were laughing our asses off, having a blast. But for Mia, it wouldn't last.

★ ★ ★

Mia's schedule in 1967 was set. First, she would shoot *Rosemary's Baby* for Paramount, and then immediately after would work with Frank on a movie he was about to do for 20th Century Fox called *The Detective*. Unfortunately, the filming of *Rosemary's Baby* went more and more slowly, and fell way behind schedule. Frank would not change his shooting schedule and was insistent that Mia "get the hell off *Rosemary's*."

I was hanging out with Mia in her pink-flowered dressing room. She was crying because she was under tremendous pressure from Frank. He told her he'd divorce her if she didn't leave.

She loved making the movie and didn't want to leave it, but she was clearly afraid of what he might do if she stayed on.

There's been a lot written about this episode; it's been told from many points of view. I'm telling it now as someone who was there, who saw the look of fear on Mia's face as she struggled with her situation.

I felt so bad for her.

Finally, Mia let Frank know she intended to finish *Rosemary's*. We were all waiting to see what Frank would do next. One day while shooting on Stage 9, Frank's lawyer Mickey Rudin showed up to deliver her divorce papers.

Mia was heartbroken.

While filming the final scene of *Rosemary's Baby*, I witnessed, along with the entire crew to our great collective horror and embarrassment, one of the loudest and most outrageous fights that to this day I have ever seen on a movie set. This one took place on Stage 18 of Paramount, on the set of the Castavet's apartment, and it happened between John Cassavetes, who played Rosemary's husband, Guy Woodhouse, and Roman.

Roman and Cassavetes loathed one another. Cassavetes, a director himself, was at odds with the way Roman worked and had made a point of making that quite clear throughout filming. Roman had spent enough time working with Cassavetes to come to the conclusion that he was a giant pain in the ass.

In the scene, Mia (as Rosemary) has figured out that something is going on in the Castavet's apartment. Through a secret passageway, she enters their apartment, and the entire coven sees her, including her husband. This is the climactic scene where she realizes, upon seeing the black-shrouded bassinet, that she has given birth to an incarnation of the devil.

It's a powerful and frightening scene. In it, Guy cowers, trying to hide from Rosemary. Cassavetes was unhappy with the way Roman blocked the scene and was especially upset with the dialogue where he tells Rosemary not to worry, that everything is okay.

The argument started slowly, but then increased to a point where Cassavetes and Roman both lost it. They hurled every invective possible at one another. The entire cast and crew were paralyzed. Seconds before they came to blows, Ruth Gordon stepped in and defused the situation, saying the equivalent of, "That's enough, boys. Let's get back to work. We've got a scene to do."

I was twenty-one years old, but I still remember the reaction of one of the electricians on the set. He said, "I've been in this business over forty years, since the silents. I've never seen or heard an argument even close to this in all that time."

13

In 1959, my parents became friends with Butch and Shirley Baskin—of those famous thirty-one flavors—because both couples were charter members of a new country club in Tarzana called El Caballero.

Butch and Shirley had two children, Edie, who was my age, and Richard, who was a few years younger than me. Our families were so close that they bought Palm Springs condominiums next door to one another. They even shared an adjoining wall. We spent a lot of time with the Baskins on weekends and holidays. Tragically, on Christmas Eve 1967, Butch died suddenly of a heart attack. Naturally, we were all devastated.

Shirley was understandably heartbroken. My mom and dad did everything they could to comfort her, but she was still at sea. It wasn't long before my father came up with an idea that would ensure Shirley would never have to be alone—at least in Palm Springs: he knocked down the common wall between our two condos, and from then on, all of us lived, played, and ate together on those Palm Springs getaways.

To this day Shirley, Edie, and Richard are family.

With that gesture, my dad demonstrated his generosity of spirit. I know of no other man who would be willing to share his life with another family by breaking down the literal wall that separated them.

I didn't understand how I could ever feel anything other than love and respect for this man. And yet I did. Carrying my father's name came with a self-imposed expectation that I needed to be just like him. In addition to the love I felt for him, the fact that I couldn't possibly live up to that expectation left me feeling vastly inferior.

* * *

After *Rosemary's Baby,* I thought it was time to leave Bill Castle. Because of the generosity of the assistant directors who taught me the ropes, I felt I was ready to become a full-fledged second AD. It's very difficult to get into the Directors Guild of America. You have to have years of nonunion experience or proof that you have worked in a Directors Guild capacity for more than ninety days. If that was the case, because of the Taft-Hartley Act, they had to let you in.

The 1947 act states that if no union members are available to do a job, a nonunion person can be hired to do that particular job. In my case, the Directors Guild gave me a waiver to work on *This Property Is Condemned* because there was nobody available to come to Louisiana and Mississippi to do the movie, and I was already down there. What the DGA didn't know was that the movie was going to shoot for 105 days, so I worked well over the ninety-day requirement, which left me eligible to join the union. I got letters confirming my work from Sydney Pollack, Clarence Eurist, and John Houseman.

My first job as second (to Dave Salven) was on a movie called *Pendulum,* a thriller starring George Peppard, Jean Seberg, and Richard Kiley. The movie was directed by George Schaefer, who'd won a lot of Emmys for television but hadn't yet directed a feature. We were set to shoot in front of a police station in Washington, DC, beginning April 5, 1968. On the evening of April 4, Martin Luther King, Jr., was assassinated.

The decision had been made to keep on schedule, so the following morning we arrived at our location, the police station, which was about five blocks from the Capitol, to begin filming, as if adhering to our schedule could force some kind of normalcy back into our lives. We tried, but I don't think our hearts were in it. I know mine wasn't.

At about three o'clock that afternoon, we were in the middle of filming a scene when a spokesperson for the police came to us and said, "You have to leave. The whole city is shutting down because a riot just broke out several blocks from here. You have to get out now."

This might have been the moment when the protective bubble—made entirely of hubris—that an all-white Los Angeles movie crew carried into an all-black city one day after MLK was assassinated—burst. We were not safe here.

Dave wrapped the company immediately and said as coolly and calmly as he could, given the circumstances, "All right, let's get George and Jean in a car. Howard, you get them back to the hotel."

We were all terrified, of course, but I had learned my whole life that my loyalty was to my job, to the movie, and to the crew. I had a responsibility, and I intended to fulfill it. In this case, if it was on me to get the actors back safely, then that's exactly what I was going to do.

Peppard, Seberg, and I got in a car, but it was immediately obvious we weren't going anywhere because the streets were completely filled. There was no way to move since all the government buildings had let out at the same time and everyone was making the same exodus we were trying to make. Dave said, "It's not gonna work. Howard, you and I will have to walk them back to the hotel."

It was two miles from the police station to our hotel. Dave and I sandwiched the two stars between us. Things seemed fairly quiet, and therefore relatively safe, for the first couple of blocks, but as we walked farther on toward our hotel, we had no other choice but to head straight into the middle of the riot. It was chaos. It was loud, windows were breaking, fires were burning, and people were running past with TVs and anything else they could loot. It was terrifying, and we had no business being in the middle of it.

We managed to move ourselves out of the center of danger and made it back to the hotel, badly shaken but safe.

We were not allowed to leave the hotel for three days as the city remained under siege. Dave placed a call to John Veitch, the head of physical production at Columbia. I was there when Dave asked John, "Given the situation here, what do you want us to do?"

I will never forget Dave telling me Veitch's response: "You're there, I'm not. I trust you to make the right decision."

That wise reply made a lasting impression on me and has informed professional and personal decisions I've either made myself or deferred to the one directly involved in a situation.

Dave gave it some thought and eventually decided, "Let's get out of here. This is no place to be making a movie right now."

Relieved that he decided to pull the plug, we all flew home, determined that whatever was left to shoot could and would be faked on the back lot of Columbia.

I learned a great lesson from my experience on *Pendulum*—from John Veitch and from Dave Salven. I learned the value of trusting the instincts of the person whose boots are on the ground. I learned the value of not deferring difficult decisions to the boss if he or she is not there experiencing whatever the challenge is. That taught me to believe in my authority, and I learned that by witnessing both John and Dave bearing the burden of their decisions in the most difficult of circumstances.

★ ★ ★

After *Pendulum*, I got a call from Hank Moonjean, who had been the first on *The Odd Couple*. He asked if I'd be his second on a movie called *The April Fools*, starring Jack Lemmon and Catherine Deneuve. I—like the rest of the world—was enchanted with her after seeing *The Umbrellas of Cherbourg*.

I called Bob Redford to tell him my news because, in 1965, when we were shooting *Property* in New Orleans, we had talked about our respective crushes on her, an admission that allowed us to share a great experience. I'd read in the New Orleans newspaper that a nearby art house was playing a double bill of *Umbrellas of Cherbourg* and *Jules et Jim*. Because we were shooting from noon to midnight,

Bob had me call the theater to ask if we could hire the projectionist to arrange for a post-midnight private showing after we wrapped.

There's a great scene in *Jules et Jim* where Jeanne Moreau is dancing down a hill toward Oskar Werner when the famous song "Le Tourbillon" comes on. When it did, Redford and I—alone in the theater—spontaneously got up and began to sing and dance as it was playing on-screen. We danced down the theater aisle, Bob on one side and me on the other, as if we were the only two people in the theater...which we were. Then the two of us sat down in the front row and watched Catherine Deneuve sing and dance all the way through *Umbrellas of Cherbourg*. It was another magic moment.

Here it is three years later, and I could barely contain my excitement when my job was to pick up Catherine Deneuve at JFK Airport.

She arrived with the famous French director Agnes Varda and one other friend. I was bubbling over with enthusiasm, and hopefully professionalism, when I said, "Hi, Miss Deneuve. I'm Howard Koch, Jr., and I'm so happy to meet you."

She granted me an obviously couldn't-be-bothered, "Hello."

Disappointed but undaunted, after leading them to the limousine, I began to explain what the schedule would be for her for the next few days. She made it patently clear that I was beneath her, and she didn't want a thing to do with me. I think Redford might have had better luck.

I learned a lot of great AD lessons from Hank Moonjean on this film and will always be grateful to him for mentoring me. Hank was always many steps ahead of everyone else on the set. To say Hank was prepared is an understatement.

Another lesson that I still use to this day is the way in which he communicated to the crew. He encouraged everyone—no matter the craft—to come to him with any question, large or small. He knew that open communication was the key to successful working relationships since that was what would best serve the film.

* * *

I did several more movies as a second AD, one of which was the seminal comedy *Bob & Carol & Ted & Alice,* Paul Mazursky's directing debut. The last one, *Cactus Flower,* gave me another opportunity to work with director Gene Saks. It starred my old pal Walter Matthau, three-time Academy Award–winner Ingrid Bergman, and Goldie Hawn in her debut movie, for which she won an Oscar. Ingrid was in her fifties by the time I worked with her, and as tough as nails, but a true professional gift to work with.

We had a great cinematographer, Charles Lang, who won an Oscar for *A Farewell to Arms* and was nominated for seventeen others. He had photographed some of the most beautiful women all through the 1930s, '40s, '50s, and into the '60s. One night I went to a screening of *The Fox,* a movie my friend Billy Fraker had photographed.

I told Charlie the next morning, "Oh, my God, I just saw one of the most beautifully photographed movies ever. Billy Fraker did it. It's called *The Fox."*

Charlie asked, "Isn't that the one with the twenty-two-year-old girl in the red dress in the snow?"

When I told him it was, he said, as though it should have been obvious to me, "I've got Ingrid Bergman who's fifty-five but wants to look twenty-five. If I can pull that off, *that's* cinematography."

I said, "Point taken, Charlie," and then I shut up.

* * *

During prep I got a call from the head of the studio who told me he wanted his son, a junior like me, to be my assistant on *Cactus Flower.* He said, "Just treat him like anybody else. Don't hold back. Don't treat him differently because I'm head of the studio and he's my son."

I assured him, "Believe me, I know exactly what you mean. Because I'm Howard W. Koch, Jr., I've had to work extra hard my whole career just to be treated like everyone else. I'll make sure your son is treated the same."

This junior had been trying to do the impossible task of living up to his famous father's name just as I had. If anyone could understand his dilemma, it was me.

The only problem was it turned out his son couldn't have cared less about the movie business. And nobody was going to fire him.

We did a big disco scene with a lot of extras. I told Junior, "I placed all the background extras either on the dance floor or at tables with the food they're eating. Make a chart so that when we move in for close-ups and go around the main table, I'll be able to call in only those we need, not all of them."

We broke for lunch, and when we came back, we were ready for coverage, so I asked him for the chart. He said, "I didn't do it."

I said, "Why not? I asked you to do it. Why didn't you?"

"Well, I got busy," he said, oozing apathy.

I was pissed because I'd been trying to mentor him. It never occurred to me that his way of dealing with being a junior might make him loathe the very business I loved and wanted to succeed in. Instead of expressing understanding, or even curiosity, I ripped into him. As we were wrapping, I got a message that his father, Mr. Head of the Studio, wanted to see me in his office.

When I arrived the first thing he said to me was, "I heard you were pretty mean to my son today."

"Well," I tried to explain, "I asked him to do something important, and he didn't do it. So, I reacted to him just like I would to anybody else, just like you told me to."

Senior replied, "I'm sure he *did* do it. He's not the kind of guy who wouldn't. You better be careful about how you handle people."

"Yes, sir," I said, happy I hadn't been fired.

One of my regrets is that I did not have the maturity to extend my compassion, instead of my judgment, to his son.

14

My sister wasn't happy in her marriage to Ben, and even though she had two little girls, she decided to get divorced in 1969. Within a year she met her second husband, Alan Blinken, who was an investment banker in New York. Alan and Melinda married in 1970 and have been together ever since.

Rita and I were both twenty-one when we got married. Kids! We had gotten a little house that we decorated together, and we were living the same trajectory as our parents. We were both working hard, she in a clothing store and me as an AD. We'd spend the weekends visiting friends or having them over to barbecue, or we'd go see either set of our parents. We were happily ensconced in building our nest and making our life together.

Before *Cactus Flower* finished, we found out Rita was pregnant, and we couldn't have been happier.

John Veitch thought I was ready to move up to first AD. My first job was on a film called *Getting Straight*, a movie starring Elliott Gould and Candice Bergen, filmed in Eugene, Oregon. This was an antiwar film that took place at a fictitious college and centered around the riots on college campuses against the Vietnam War. Elliott played a radical teacher who stood up for what he believed in. We were shooting in Eugene in July when Neil Armstrong landed on the moon. About an hour after watching "one small step for man, one giant leap for mankind," on a TV in a bar, Elliott, Candy, and I found ourselves in a car driving to Florence, Oregon, because it had great beaches with sand dunes and seemed like the perfect place to contemplate the moon landing. We got a little stoned and were lying on the beach looking up at the full moon, each of us gobsmacked with the wildest realization (nicely enhanced by the pot) that, "Wow—there's a man walking up there right now!" It was an absolutely mind-blowing and wonderful historic moment to share with Elliott and Candy.

After *Getting Straight*, I got a job as the AD on *The Baby Maker*, for first-time director James Bridges, who'd also written the screenplay. Jim went on to direct *The Paper Chase, The China Syndrome,* and *Urban Cowboy.*

The Baby Maker was the story of a couple who couldn't have a baby due to the wife's infertility, so they decided to use the husband's sperm to impregnate a surrogate. They've made a deal that once it's born, the baby will go to the husband and wife, but by the time the surrogate is ready to give birth, her feelings have become complicated, and she doesn't want to give the baby up.

Those were the days when Lamaze was first becoming popular, and in the film, the husband, wife, and birth mother go to classes together. In true "art imitates life" fashion, Rita and I were taking Lamaze classes too, even though the hospital where Rita would be giving birth didn't yet allow fathers in the delivery room. The classes didn't do a lot for me since I couldn't be her coach as fathers can today, but they did help Rita learn to breathe.

On November 17, 1969, Rita called the doctor because she thought something was happening. Although he asked her to wait a bit longer, I got another call from her at twelve thirty. When she said, "The doctor said I should go to the hospital now," I morphed into Ricky Ricardo in that famous episode where Lucy calmly announces she's ready to have the baby and suddenly Ricky, who's practiced this moment a million times, starts running around like his pants are on fire.

"I'm leaving right this second. I'll be there in twenty minutes—or less," I stuttered before jumping in the car and racing home to pick her up. We drove to Cedars of Lebanon Hospital. Since she was having major contractions by then, I dropped her off in front of the hospital entrance where she was met and escorted by a nurse.

When I arrived upstairs moments later, I asked, "Where is my wife, Rita Koch?" To my surprise, the nurse replied, "Oh, she's already in delivery!"

I sprinted to the waiting room and saw that Rita's parents and my mother had already arrived. My father couldn't come because he had a cold, so he was waiting eagerly at home for the call.

The three of us waited and waited. When it seemed like forever had finally arrived, the doc came in and announced, "It's a boy!" at which point all four of us burst into tears. We called my father from the payphone right outside the waiting room. I never saw my father cry, but I know he must have when Billy, his first grandson and his father's namesake, was born.

When Billy came home, it was the most exciting time of our lives. He was an easy and wonderful baby. Sometimes I would sit in a rocking chair, with him lying on my chest, patting him on his back to help him go to sleep. I loved him beyond my ability to imagine love. He was my first child, my son, and that's an experience that brings incomparable joy. Life was good.

★　★　★

Looking back through a more current lens, I can see how naïve and inappropriate my expectations about parenting were. But I didn't know that then. I did not know—and, given my history, was emotionally unprepared for—the extent to which when a woman becomes a mother, the baby eclipses everything, including the husband, who recedes into the background. Since the background was the very place from which I had spent most of my life trying to extricate myself, my marital demotion was difficult. Regrettably, my understanding when I first became a father was the only one available to me at the time.

Even though it was entirely unconscious, I think I (foolishly) expected that my wife would treat me like the only couple I had ever witnessed: the way my mother treated my dad. My mother always put her husband's needs first. Maybe I hadn't noticed that by the late '60s when Billy was born, things were entirely different.

Rita and I were each separately working our assess off—she fully engrossed in being Billy's mother, and I, as the provider, continuing to work hard on whatever movie I was lucky enough to be on.

A pattern developed where I'd come home after a full day's work to find Rita, tired from caring for our energetic young son, asleep in bed, having left me a warm plate of food for dinner. Where was the woman who refreshed her makeup and put on a dress and heels as my mother did? Oh right, wrong decade.

On weekends we'd do things together as a family but that little time we shared wasn't enough to assuage my growing sense of insignificance and my familiar feeling of loneliness, a loneliness I thought I'd left behind when I got married.

Even though I had a booming professional voice (on the set my nickname was "Bullhorn" because I was so loud that I didn't need one), I didn't have a clue how to express myself at home. I didn't realize that my uncommunicative style and brewing discontent were harbingers of trouble in our marriage.

As always seemed to happen, the phone rang, offering not just a job but the perfect excuse for not dealing with my personal struggles.

I was offered a job in West Virginia on a movie called *Fools' Parade* that was being directed by Andy McLaglen, a fine director for whom I would work again.

James Stewart and George Kennedy were the stars of the movie, along with Kurt Russell, who was an up-and-comer at the time. I was personally awed to be able to work with James Stewart near the end of his career. I must have watched *Mr. Smith Goes to Washington, The Philadelphia Story,* and *It's a Wonderful Life* hundreds of times.

I had spent my life around movie stars and celebrities, yet there were still times—like this one—when I'd pinch myself standing next to the camera saying, "My God, I'm actually on a set watching Jimmy Stewart perform!" I've continued to be grateful for the opportunity I've had to work with such immense talents throughout my career.

15

When I got back from location, Rita and I hosted a backyard Father's Day barbecue. She made the salads, while I handled the meat, having become quite fond of barbecuing over the years.

Both sets of our parents were there, along with Rita's sisters and a few other guests. No doubt my dad was wearing his favorite plaid pants with the orange belt. (No one ever accused him of having good taste in clothes.) Billy was all dressed up and running around, secure in his role as the boy everyone loved to love. He was lapping up the attention of all the doting adults as only a year-and-a-half-year-old could do. I'd made an early trip to Pink's to pick up enough chili to slather over our hot dogs and hamburgers. To complete the happy picture, our beagle, Kluny, who we'd gotten as a puppy, was trying his best to guilt the guests into sharing their food.

I'm sure Rita and I displayed quite an enviable image of a happy couple, but the truth was I wasn't happy inside. I might have had a flicker of awareness that day, but it would have been such a little flicker that it would have slipped back down into my subconscious before the tossed burger had a chance to land back down on the spatula. And then I would have smiled at our guests and eaten way too much.

Like most people in the business of making movies, I was working a schedule not particularly conducive to family life. Not only are the professional hours difficult, but if you are away on location, like I so often was, you really need a maturity and strength of character that I didn't possess in my twenties. I'm not proud of the fact that back then, the way I dealt with being unhappy at home was to compartmentalize and rationalize being unfaithful. I made a lot of mistakes that you can't make if you're going to stay married. Because I had learned to keep so much to myself, it never occurred to me to discuss my marriage with anyone, even though in retrospect, I wish that my father and I had had the kind of relationship that would have made those conversations possible.

Soon I got a call from Doc Merman, the head of physical production at Fox. They were firing the first AD on a movie called *Billy Jack*, which was both starring and being directed by Tom Laughlin. One of my first assignments was to find a nude double for his wife, who was co-starring, for a scene scheduled to shoot the next day. Of the twenty-five women standing outside the Ramada Inn in Santa Fe, New Mexico, hoping to get the part, I was to pick the one who looked the best naked and the most like his wife. This was no easy task because although I couldn't say what Delores looked like naked, it was pretty obvious from seeing her with her clothes on that she was neither curvaceous nor endowed with large breasts, as many of these women were. Delores had a slim figure, reminiscent of Popeye's girlfriend, Olive Oyl. Delores was petite, about five-foot-four and had long, dark brown hair. I asked the few similarly built contenders to remove their clothes. I picked the one from among them who I thought would most resemble Delores and could most easily be her double.

When I showed Tom the woman, he was annoyed and snapped, "She doesn't look a thing like my wife! What about that one over there?"

"That one over there" was a five-ten blonde, easily fifteen years younger than Delores, and well endowed. I asked her if she'd please remove her clothes, whereupon Tom asserted, "She's going to be my wife's double!" If this wasn't a lesson in beauty being in the eye of the beholder, I don't know what is. Oh, and there was another lesson: the director is always right!

* * *

While I was in Santa Fe, Peter Fonda came to town to prep a movie he was going to direct called *The Hired Hand*. He had just produced and starred in *Easy Rider*, one of the seminal movies of the 1960s. I was thrilled when he asked me to be his first AD.

We were on a location scout one day driving around in Peter's Chevy Blazer looking for a riverbed in which to shoot a particular scene. We parked the Blazer and were walking along when all of a sudden, we heard a rattlesnake. I jumped twenty feet in the air. But not Peter. He took out his buck knife, circled around behind the rattler, and with a move faster than the Karate Kid, chopped its head right off. Just when I thought he couldn't get any cooler, he did.

Peter wanted his friend László Kovács, who had shot *Easy Rider*, to photograph *The Hired Hand*, but László was unavailable. Instead, László recommended his friend Vilmos Zsigmond for the job and Peter hired him.

László and Vilmos were both photojournalists in Hungary. Together they chronicled the events of the 1956 Hungarian Revolution on thirty thousand feet of film. They snuck under a fence—with the footage—to escape Hungary when the Russians wouldn't let anybody out. They shared the kind of experience that makes men brothers.

Filming *The Hired Hand* was a big opportunity for Vilmos. There are a few DPs whom I've worked with over my fifty years in the business that I would say were true artists, and Vilmos was one of them. He went on to photograph *McCabe & Mrs. Miller, The Deer Hunter*, and *Close Encounters of the Third Kind*, for which he won an Oscar. I got to work with Vilmos again when I produced *Sliver* more than twenty years later.

* * *

Producer Stanley Jaffe called and asked me to AD his film *Bad Company*, starring Jeff Bridges and directed by first-time director

Robert Benton. (He and his writing partner David Newman had written *Bonnie and Clyde*.)

During prep, Stanley asked me to go to the airport to pick up our cinematographer, Gordon Willis. He was known as the "prince of darkness" and had just finished photographing *The Godfather*.

Just as I was leaving, Stanley laughingly informed me, "By the way, he eats assistant directors for lunch."

All the way to the airport I was convincing myself that Stanley was kidding. But I knew I was screwed when, after introducing myself to Gordon with a warm, "Hi, I'm Howard, the first AD, and I'm happy to be working with you," he didn't reply. I cut him a little slack, but no matter how much time passed I received nothing but radio silence.

I was tap-dancing inside my head until I decided to say, "We've got a little time before our first meeting. Are you hungry?"

I struck gold because when he said, "Where can I get a great hamburger?" he had no idea he'd asked one of the world's greatest burger aficionados. Within a half hour the two of us were laughing and enjoying the first of many Apple Pan hickory smoked cheeseburgers.

Gordon Willis taught me one of the greatest film lessons I ever learned. Two weeks before shooting, Gordon, dog-eared script in hand, sat Benton and me down for a couple of hours every night. He wanted to know Benton's vision of every single scene and every transition from scene to scene.

For example, in referring to scene one, he would ask, "Do you want it static or moving? Do you want it close or far back? Do you want it high or low?"

He left no stone unturned. I felt like I received a PhD in the art and importance of preparation in those two weeks. I came away fully aware of what the director and the director of photography were after. That lesson has served me well on every movie I have made since, whether I was working as an AD or later as a producer. Oh, and knowing where to get a great hamburger doesn't hurt either.

I never got to work with Benton again, but he went on to win two Oscars for *Kramer vs. Kramer* (for best adapted screenplay and best director). Stanley Jaffe produced *Kramer,* which won him an Oscar for Best Picture.

16

My personal life seemed to be unraveling in direct proportion to how confident I felt in my professional life. This incongruity became harder and harder for me to reconcile. I was leading an interesting and fulfilling life as an AD. I was in control of everything on the set of multimillion-dollar movies. I knew I was a capable and respected AD, but at home it seemed as if I couldn't do anything right. And maybe I couldn't.

I always wanted to have children, and in contrast to how I was raised, I wanted to participate in their lives. But from the backseat position I occupied at home, it was easy to convince me that I didn't know what I was doing when it came to being Billy's father.

Over time I found myself wondering how I could feel so good on set and so bad and alone at home.

On some of those nights when I'd come home late from work and would be eating alone in the kitchen, I would think about my marriage and how Rita and I were basically kids who were doing what was expected of us and what we expected of ourselves: get married, have a baby, and be just like our parents. But was I really like my parents? Did I want to be like them or did I want to be myself? And who was that anyway? I felt like I was playacting at marriage.

Soon enough I was away on another movie and acutely aware of the lingering notion that I was much happier working than I was at home. One night after I returned home from location, Rita could tell something was wrong.

"What is it?"

"I don't know if it's the right thing for us to do, but I've been thinking about moving out because neither one of us is happy. We need a change. I think we should try a trial separation."

True to our inability to discuss anything of consequence, Rita didn't have a big reaction. There was just a vast silence and sadness that followed, maybe even resignation.

Soon after that conversation, I had rented a small apartment in West Hollywood and began my life as a single man—albeit one whose heart was broken about his son.

It was my newfound bachelorhood that became the source of a feeling with which I had no familiarity at all up till then: guilt. I was wracked with it for being separated and for making a choice that went against everything I'd known growing up. My parents were happily married for more than sixty years; Rita's stayed together forever too.

I was seesawing between a solid conviction that I was doing the right thing, while being utterly plagued with doubt. I didn't know who I was or what I wanted.

Right about this time I was hired to AD a movie called *Up the Sandbox,* starring Barbra Streisand. It would be filmed in LA, New York, and Africa. I was happy to be getting back to work to take my mind off my personal problems.

Our director was Irvin Kershner, who would many years later direct *Star Wars: The Empire Strikes Back.* And once again I got to work with Gordon Willis.

When it was time to move the crew east for the New York portion of our film, I was surprised to make a connection to a woman I met on the flight. In addition to her obvious interest in me, I found her kind, and we began to see one another. Being with her helped clarify that I was making the right decision about my separation.

Even though I'd been in New York no more than a few weeks, I was beginning to sense that it was possible for me to be just as happy off the set as I was on it, that my personal life could be as fulfilling as my professional life was.

And then I got the call: Rita was pregnant.

The word "tailspin" took on an all-new and personal meaning for me, but I didn't have time to do much about it because I had to fly to Africa to shoot the fantasy sequence for *Up the Sandbox,* and by now, I had pretty much perfected the art of compartmentalizing.

Kersh, our director, had lost the fight that would have allowed him, Gordon, and me to scout for locations in Kenya before the shoot. It was risky, but we'd just have to see them when we got there.

We were driven straight to the Mount Kenya Safari Club, which was the equivalent of a five-star hotel. The valet parkers and bellhops were dressed in perfectly ironed khaki shorts with a uniform short-sleeved shirt and a hat.

The grounds were lush and impeccably manicured, verdant under the watchful eye of Mount Kenya.

The rooms were just as stunningly beautiful—rich, dark wood, with all the luxuries you could imagine. We took showers and went downstairs to meet for a mind-boggling meal they called dinner.

As if all this weren't enough to convince me I was in heaven, I returned to my room to find that my clothes had been cleaned and folded and that the sheets on my bed were warmed. And to think, everything I've just described fell under the heading of work!

The following morning, we were driven to the predetermined site of our location by a tribal chief wearing a US Army cutoff shirt. He was a friendly and talkative guy who regaled us with stories of his work on *King Solomon's Mines* and his friendship with the director Andrew "Boomy" Marton. He was positive we were going to love the locations that had been chosen for us, but we were skeptical.

It was a ten-minute drive up into the stunning mountains of Mount Kenya where we saw beautiful pine trees. There was only one teeny (read: insurmountable) problem: who'd pay to go all the way to another continent to shoot pine trees that looked exactly like what we'd see in Colorado? We knew immediately this wouldn't work for our fantasy sequence with Barbra and the French Senegalese dancers we had hired.

After telling the producer we couldn't possibly shoot there, the three of us went in search of an appropriate location.

By now the crew had arrived. They suffered through the next three days sitting around the unspeakably beautiful Mount Kenya Safari Club, with nothing to do but enjoy the beauty that is Kenya. I'm sure each and every one of them was forever changed by having had that once-in-a-lifetime experience.

During our scout, we came upon an area called Samburu. The landscape was perfect for the sequence. It was expansive, arid, and spotted with beautiful acacia trees. In it, we found a small nomadic village with huts made of cow dung, mud, and sticks, and about seventy-five tribespeople who seemed perfect for our sequence. We knew immediately we had found our location. They were warm and friendly people, who, after we began working together, dubbed me "Kochey."

About a half-hour drive from the village was the Samburu Game Lodge. It was a perfect place to house the cast and crew with the minor exception that since it was small, the crew would have to stay two and three to a room. Well, except for Barbra of course.

Barbra was and is extraordinarily attached to her comforts. She's also funny, smart, passionate about her work, and a consummate professional. She brings you in, and she wants to discuss and ask questions about the work. She wants to make sure that what ends up on film is exactly what you came there to get.

There was a moment during our first visit to the village when a group of Samburu children started singing for us. Barbra was so moved that she spontaneously began to sing and to improvise with them. Not only was it as beautiful as you can imagine, it was poignantly touching. These little kids had no idea who Barbra was. She knew it and took comfort in a rare noncelebrity moment. She wasn't singing with them for any other reason than the pure and contagious joy of beautiful voices joining one another in song.

My experience with celebrities is that because they have so little privacy, they tend to hold back when they're with people they don't know, especially if those people have some expectation of the star persona. But when on the rare occasions they're with people who aren't aware of their stardom and don't have any expectations, then they're free to be themselves. In that moment with the kids in Samburu, Barbra was free, and it was beautiful to witness.

We had a great prop man with us, Alan Levine, who during prep had discussed with Kersh how many spears he might need to have on hand for the fantasy sequence. Kersh assured him fifty would be plenty.

When we got to the Samburu village to shoot, instead of the expected seventy-five tribespeople, there were at least three hundred. They'd learned of the movie production via village-to-village drumming. We were thrilled knowing it was going to be an impressive sequence, except that once again we had one tiny problem—the kind of tiny problem that seems to go hand in hand with moviemaking. This time the problem was we had agreed on only fifty spears, so that's all Alan had.

Kersh, in his typical guilelessness, turned to Alan and said, "I need more spears."

Alan, who had a mouth like an angry sailor, hurled back: "More spears? Really? And just where the fuck do you think I'm going to get more spears? In case you hadn't noticed, we're in the middle of fucking nowhere. You son of a bitch. I'm outta here!"

He got in a Land Rover with his driver and stormed off, kicking up a trail of dust as they drove away.

We went on prepping the big shot without Alan. Sometime later we were set up and almost ready to roll. I had fifty spears with the guys in the foreground, trying to hide the fact that the guys in the background didn't have spears.

Stating the obvious, Kersh said to me, "I wish we had spears in the back."

"I do too, Kersh, but we don't. This is the best we're gonna do so let's go."

"Oh, all right," he said, finally resigned.

Just before calling action we heard a *Toot toot, toot, toot.* I saw a dust tail approaching, but I didn't know who the hell was honking and about to ruin our shot, when up drove Alan Levine in his Land Rover with literally hundreds of spears sticking out the back. Many hundreds of them! He got out of the car, went to the back, and started launching spears at Kersh.

"You want spears, Kersh?" *Launch.* "Here's your spears!" *Launch.* "Take your goddamn spears, Kersh." *Launch.*

"Shoot your fucking movie. And it damn well better be good!" *Launch, launch, launch.*

I don't know where he got them, but I do know that Alan was one of the greatest prop men/magicians ever.

17

Despite the beauty of and adventures in Africa, the news that Rita was pregnant weighed heavily on me, and I continued to suffer with the dilemma of what to do. Before flying home at the end of the job, I contracted a stomach parasite and got quite ill. By the time I left Africa and arrived back in New York City, I looked like hell. I'd lost fifteen pounds in five days. The layover between the Nairobi–London and London–New York flights was so short that my luggage never made the connection.

When I said to the customs guy, "I must look like hell," he snarked back, "What you look like is a smuggler. Come with me."

They took me into a room and poked and probed every sorry orifice of mine despite my protestations and insistence that I had been making a movie in Africa and had gotten sick five days prior.

It wasn't until I dropped the magic words "We're making the movie with Barbra Streisand, and she'll be returning on this very flight tomorrow" that they tossed aside all their suspicions about me. Not only did they let me go, but when my luggage did arrive, they sent it to me unopened. I could have been bringing in anything. That's how I knew I was back home, in the land where celebrity trumps just about everything else.

★ ★ ★

As I was finishing *Up the Sandbox*, I got a call from my friend Sydney Pollack, asking if I was available to work with him on his next project, *The Way We Were*. Working with people you've worked with before, whose idiosyncrasies you're familiar with, always makes an AD's life easier. Because I'd already worked with Sydney, Barbra, Redford, and producer Ray Stark, I felt validated that Sydney would ask me again.

The script was still being worked on during prep, this time by Alvin Sargent. The original idea and screenplay were by Arthur Laurents, who in the end got sole screen credit, although had I been an arbiter, I certainly would have included Alvin Sargent's pass on the script. It made a huge difference to the final outcome. And of course, Sydney always had his script doctor David Rayfiel standing by.

One day, during prep, Sydney asked me to stay in his office because he was having a meeting with, as he put it, "Some young composer who's got music he wants to play."

A tall, gangly, awkward, and visibly nervous young guy entered the office. "Hi, uh, hi, wow, Sydney Pollack, it's so exciting to meet you."

He went on nervously, "So listen, I read the script, and I couldn't afford an orchestra so I taped myself playing the piano and I've written the theme that I think should be your theme for this movie. I'll play the horns with my mouth, but you'll have to imagine what real horns would sound like. I just want you to hear it." He was sweet, but given that opening, we sure didn't expect much.

He finished his speech with a humble, "Thanks so much for seeing me," and then he proceeded to hit play on a tiny little tape recorder. As the music was beginning, he pressed his lips together and out came a pretty impressive horn sound. From the moment I heard the first notes—Da da...da da da da da da dada—chills ran up and down my spine. It was hauntingly beautiful. Sydney, looking equally moved, thanked the young man sincerely and asked him as he was walking out the door, "What's your name again?"

He said shyly, "Oh, it's Marvin. Marvin Hamlisch."

After Marvin got hired, the music was given to Barbra's friends, Marilyn and Alan Bergman, who wrote the beautiful lyrics. The score and song each won an Oscar.

Our plan was to shoot the college sequences first in Schenectady, New York, then move to New York City, then do all the Los Angeles locations and sets. Once winter hit New York, we'd go back for the final scene outside the Plaza Hotel. No matter how many films I've worked on in my life, or directors or stars I've worked with, being Sydney Pollack's first AD will always remain a highlight of my career. As happens with films like *The Way We Were,* everyone working on it knew it was going to be special.

One day while shooting in Schenectady, the Teamsters invited all the bigwigs of the movie, including Barbra, Bob, and Sydney, to have a personally prepared Italian dinner. The Teamsters, all Italian, were made up of fathers and their sons. It was the young Teamsters who picked us up in cars outside our hotel at seven that evening. I happened to be riding with Barbra, and as the drive got longer and longer and we headed into an area that was darker and darker, and I must admit, a bit foreboding, Barbra began to worry. I made sure to hide my concerns from her.

She said with a Brooklyn edge, "Where are you taking me? The food better be good!"

We turned the corner and there on a dark street was one brightly lit sign that said "Luncheonette"—looking like something out of an Edward Hopper painting.

Barbra, concerned, whispered to me, "Are you sure this place is safe?"

"Of course, it is," I lied.

We went in, and to our great relief, we ended up having an amazing twelve-course meal prepared for us by the young Teamsters' Italian fathers and uncles, while their aunts, wives, and sisters served. Everyone was relaxed and enjoyed themselves until well past midnight. We all loved the food, Barbra included, and we left feeling touched by the Teamsters' generous gesture.

It wasn't until the time cards went in that week that we learned it wasn't as generous a gesture as we originally thought. Turns out all the Teamsters on the movie, even the ones who had nothing to do with the dinner, put in their time cards from six o'clock that morning till after one o'clock the following day when we were driven home. Needless to say, that was one expensive dinner. The lesson I learned was this: clarify, always clarify, or be prepared to eat it.

★ ★ ★

Redford was letting me stay at his beach house for a little while until I rented an apartment of my own. I was anguished about my marriage. I had gotten married at twenty-one, and five years later I had one child and was separated from my wife, who was pregnant with our second child. What was I gonna do?

I was clear that I did not want to move back only to resume the shared but lonely life Rita and I had been living before our separation. But I didn't know if either of us was capable of transforming ourselves, and therefore our marriage, into a fulfilling partnership. I was utterly lost and nowhere near knowing what to do about our baby that was due in December.

I was mulling my options. Rita and I were barely communicating, which made for painful interactions for both of us when it came to the time I spent with Billy.

You never know what might break the spell of inertia. In my case, even though I'd been seesawing back and forth for a long time, the proverbial straw that broke the camel's back was a scene from *The Way We Were* that we were shooting in a little house on Malibu Road. Barbra's character, Katie Morosky, is seven months pregnant. When we rolled camera, she looked into Bob's eyes and asked earnestly, "Will you do me one favor, Hubbell? Stay with me till the baby's born."

That line shot an arrow directly into my heart, and I knew right then and there that if Rita would let me, I was moving home.

I moved back in October 1972, after Rita and I resolved to try and make our marriage work.

The baby was due December 10, which I remember because we had two more days of shooting left in New York, and they were scheduled for November 28 and 29, a Monday and Tuesday. Rita didn't want me to go in case the baby came early but—with a hubris that only hindsight allows me to acknowledge—I was confident the baby would wait until its due date. I flew to New York on Sunday, November 27, to finish the movie.

On Monday morning, November 28, 1972, we were on the set ready to shoot. All of a sudden one of the bellmen came running out to me excitedly, yelling for all the world to hear, "Mr. Koch, you've just had a baby girl!"

It was a surreal experience. Everyone burst out in applause and congratulations—so happy for me. My first reaction was complete shock, which was quickly followed by a rush of shame. I hated myself for not being there when my daughter was born. Even so, I felt utter joy just knowing I had a daughter.

Once I got home, I drove right to the hospital to meet my own personal infant heart-tugger, my precious daughter, Emily Anne Koch.

I took one look at her little face and knew immediately that from here on out I was going to make my marriage work so that I could be the best father to my two beautiful children.

18

Filming *The Parallax View*, in 1973, starring Warren Beatty and directed by Alan Pakula, was powerful and timely. Shot in the not-too-distant wake of Bobby Kennedy's death, the film dealt with the assassination of a presidential nominee, and it asked the question of whether or not it was a conspiracy or a lone assassin.

Alan Pakula, who had produced *To Kill a Mockingbird,* helmed *Klute,* and would go on to direct *All the President's Men,* had hired Gordon Willis. For the third time in as many years, I would get to work with Gordy. Additionally, I was going to be working with a great production manager, Charlie Maguire.

By now I was one of the top ADs in the business. I was being paid well to do work I could not have enjoyed more. I organized and ran a set with a confidence in my abilities that I didn't feel anywhere else in my life. We had a great crew, and as always happens, we became a family.

Everyone who's worked on a movie is painfully familiar with the expression "Hurry up and wait," since it's an understatement to say there is a lot of downtime on film sets. In the case of filming *The Parallax View,* however, the Senate hearings on Watergate were being telecast. Every time there was a break on set, we'd run to the nearest television to bring ourselves up to date on the hearings.

In true "art imitates life" fashion, our movie, which dealt with conspiracy theories, opens with a Warren Commission–type decision declaring that a prior political assassination had been committed by a lone gunman.

This story had tremendous relevance for me because not only was I deeply affected by the Kennedys assassinations, but I've never believed that all three historic icons of our modern world—John F. Kennedy, Martin Luther King, Jr., and Robert Kennedy—were killed by lone gunmen.

The political overtones that *The Parallax View* explored made working on this film all the more meaningful for me, especially because it was being made at a time of such heightened presidential corruption.

This was my life now: I was working and doing the best I could at being married. On the weekends I'd spend my time with Rita and the kids. Emily was a year old now, and Billy was four. I was fully aware that there was a hole in my life, but I had made the choice to have an intact family.

As usual, an offer of another movie relieved me of the burden to look any deeper into that hole. There was no time for that because I was going to get to run away and join the movie circus once again.

I was excited when I was called to attend two meetings for Paramount Pictures on the same day. The first was with John Schlesinger and Jerome Hellman, who had directed and produced *Midnight Cowboy*, one of my favorites.

They interviewed me about being the first AD on *The Day of the Locust*. At the end of the meeting, they offered me the job. I was excited and told them I would confirm after my next meeting with the head of the studio, Robert Evans.

When I arrived in Bob's office, he said, "Surprise—guess who's here?"

It was Roman Polanski. This turned out to be less of an interview and more them telling me the details of my next job.

"We're about five months away from filming, but we want you to start now. You and Dickie [Sylbert, the production designer and twin brother of Paul] will prep and find locations while we work on the script with the writer, Bob Towne."

I hesitated and then told Bob I had just been asked to do *Day of the Locust.*

"You're not doing that. I'm the head of the studio. You're doing *Chinatown.*"

Not only did he run the studio, but Bob was also producing *Chinatown,* so there was nothing to say but yes. I was thrilled to be working with Roman again. It was the first time he was directing in America since his wife, Sharon Tate, was murdered by Charles Manson's followers.

Roman is right up there at the top of my list of favorites, along with Sydney Pollack and Robert Benton. Technically, nobody came close to Roman's filmmaking ability. He was an incomparable auteur, and I couldn't wait to work with him again.

After reading the 180-page first draft of the script, Dick and I went out every day scouting locations. These were the days before location managers, but with Dick's keen sense of style and my geographic knowledge of Los Angeles, we managed to find every one.

I've always loved making a shooting schedule. Even though I wasn't an AD on *Rosemary's Baby,* I had learned how Roman worked and knew it was better for him psychologically to have more time than he needed. I felt the movie would take about twelve weeks to shoot, so I gave him an extra two weeks of padding. We actually shot the movie in twelve and a half weeks, and for the first time in his career, Roman was proud of finishing ahead of schedule.

Every Friday night Roman liked to wrap by six thirty so he could host a party at his house. One particularly memorable Friday we were shooting the scene where Jake was at the Department of Water and Power looking at all the photos on the wall. It was a difficult shot because we were panning from Jack Nicholson's face to one photograph, then back to his face, then back again to a different photograph. It took some time to set the focus marks.

Earlier in the week, Jack had said, "Hey, Bullhorn, you do know that Friday night the Lakers are playing the Celtics in Boston, in a big game, right? Do you have a TV set for me?"

My nickname was "Bullhorn" because my voice was so loud and deep that I didn't need the one item that seemed to be an appendage for most assistant directors.

I said, "Sure, I've got a little black-and-white Sony with rabbit ears. I'll bring it from home for you."

On that Friday afternoon, I plugged it into his knockdown trailer on the set—sort of like a little box dressing room. While we were setting up the next shot, the Lakers game was on. Since they were playing in Boston, tipoff was probably four thirty LA time. It was now more than two hours later, the fourth quarter of the game, and we were ready to shoot. I told my second AD, Michelle Ader, to go and get Jack.

When she returned without him, she told me Jack had said, "Hang on a minute. It's almost the end of the game."

Roman was none too happy hearing that because (a) we were ready to shoot the last shot of the day, and (b) it was a Friday, and he wanted to go home to his party. I sent Michelle back again. She knocked on the door, but this time Jack didn't even bother to open it.

Instead, he screamed through it, "Not yet—there's just a few seconds left!"

Roman, not amused and with eyebrows beginning to furrow, said, "Come on, Howie. You go get him."

I went this time and pleaded, "Come on, man. We gotta shoot!"

"I can't—there's thirty seconds left in the game."

And then he yelled, thrilled, "Oh, my God! Jerry West just hit a shot. We're in *overtime!*"

When I went back and told Roman, he stormed down to Jack's trailer, but Jack locked the door before he could get in.

Everyone on the set was aware of what was going on, and we were all within earshot of Roman beseeching, "Come on, Jack. We need to go. I've got a big party tonight. Mariachis, Mexican theme, you're gonna love it. Come on, we're all gonna have a great time, so let's get this shot done."

It was late and our crew—just like the Lakers and Celtics—were also going into overtime. Despite Roman's pleading, Jack was not coming out. Then we heard from inside the locked trailer, "Oh, my God—*second* overtime!"

Now Roman was screaming, but Jack refused to open the door. Finally, Roman conceded, "Okay, forget it. I'll come and watch the game with you. Then we go. Please, let me in."

"You sure, Roman?"

"Yes, let's watch it together."

Jack unlocked the door and opened it. There sat the offending TV, just inside the door and within arm's reach of Roman. He reached in, grabbed my little Sony, and slammed it across the stage floor, shattering it to smithereens.

Calling Jack's response a "blue streak" doesn't really capture it, but let's just say I learned some words I don't even think sailors had heard before. And because even that wasn't enough to release the full expression of his fury, Jack took off his suit jacket and threw it at Roman. Roman—pissed to the ceiling himself—swore back, took his sweater off, and threw it at Jack. They were screaming at each other and hurling their clothes one item at a time until they were both down to their underwear and bare feet, at which point the two of them stormed off the set in different directions.

Since it was clear we would not be shooting the scene, I yelled, "Wrap!" and wound my way up to Roman's for the party, not entirely sure there'd be one.

I braced myself for the worst but found Jack and Roman laughing and buddy-slapping each other, suddenly the best of friends.

"What happened?" I asked, befuddled.

"We got to the corner of Melrose and Gower, looked at each other in our cars—naked—and suddenly realized how hysterically ridiculous the whole thing was."

And that was that—at least until the next morning when at ten, Roman's assistant pulled up to my house and delivered a new Sony television set, courtesy of Roman. And this one was in color!

19

One of the thrills of shooting on the stage of a studio—like Paramount back in the day—is getting to see what's happening on the other stages. We were filming *Chinatown* on the west side of the lot. One day we were doing the famous scene where Jack slaps Faye Dunaway, and she reveals, "She's my sister *and* my daughter."

On the stage right next to us, John Schlesinger was shooting *Day of the Locust.* Francis Ford Coppola was shooting the Senate hearing room scene from *Godfather: Part II* on the stage right across from us.

All three sets broke for lunch at the same time, creating a parade of Hollywood A-listers: Roman Polanski, Francis Coppola, John Schlesinger, Jack Nicholson, Faye Dunaway, Al Pacino, Michael V. Gazzo, and on and on, all walking down the road together headed to the commissary to grab a bite. To add to the enchantment, all the actors and extras were in costumes representing the different eras of their films. It was a once-in-a-lifetime, spine-tingling, magical moment for this movie fan and one that I will never forget.

Jack and I were walking next to one another, silently taking it all in. We looked at each other in the same instant. Both our expressions seemed to say, "Oh, my God, look where we are." Jack broke the silence between us in that inimitable voice of his and said, "Bullhorn, we're in Hollywood!"

* * *

One of the many important moments in *Chinatown* is when Jake is trying to figure out why one place in Los Angeles has water but another is totally dry. He starts to understand when he sees the runoff at a reservoir he visits, realizing that the Department of Water and Power is withholding water from the San Fernando Valley. It's in that lightbulb moment that Jake is confronted by Roman Polanski, playing one of the heavies wielding a knife.

Roman grabs Jake and asks, "You know what happens to nosy fellas? Wanna guess? No? They lose their noses!"

Roman wanted the camera to be over the shoulder of his character and onto Jake so the viewer could actually see the knife going into his nose, watching the knife pull up to cut, followed by blood spurting out. While it was a great idea creatively, Jack was a bit nervous about how they were going to pull off the ruse without him getting injured.

We had all kinds of makeup and special effects people trying to figure it out, but everyone was stumped.

I'll never forget Roman saying in his Polish accent, "Okay, I do it. I take care of it."

And he did! He came up with the ingenious idea of putting a hinge on the end of the knife. He could actually put the tip of the knife in Jack's nose, and as he pulled up, the knife would hinge and not hurt Jack's nose at all. On the off-camera side of the knife, there was a little tube that ran down to Roman's hand. It had a little bladder filled with blood so he could squeeze it. At the right moment, the blood would run up the tube and squirt both ways over Jack's nose. Jack also had a tube running up from his feet to his hands, so when he raised his hands to grab his nose, special effects could pump more blood. Pretty brilliant but it—naturally—made Jack nervous since it was his nose.

Roman kept assuring him, "It will be okay, Jack. It will."

The first take was absolutely perfect, but given this was way before video, we couldn't play it back and therefore couldn't be sure.

We knew we couldn't risk having only one take, so we kept on shooting. While not entirely successful at hiding the smirk of enjoyment he was feeling at Jack's discomfort, Roman continued to ask for more and still more takes. With each one, Jack got increasingly more nervous, and by the twelfth take, he'd had had it.

"Enough! That's enough!" he insisted, pissed off and tired.

The one you see in the movie is take number one.

* * *

John Alonzo replaced Stanley Cortez, our DP, who had been a top cinematographer nominated for an Oscar in the 1940s for Orson Welles's *The Magnificent Ambersons*. As we began to prep the movie in 1973, we realized that Stanley was still lighting and using equipment he'd used thirty years earlier.

We knew we had some problems but one morning things came to a head—literally. We had lost a lot of time lighting the scene where Jack and Faye were sitting in a restaurant booth the morning after Jack's nose had been cut. It was a fifty-fifty, two-shot dialogue scene. Nerves were slightly frayed because this was the first scene of the day and it took Stanley so long to light that it was already close to eleven o'clock. Just as we're about to roll the camera, one hair on Faye's head popped up and the way it was lit made it look like a spear was coming directly out of the top of her head.

Roman said, "Uh, Faye, there's one hair that's popped up, and it looks like a spear. Can you mat it down or something?"

Faye pushed the hair down, unconcerned, and just as we're about to roll, up it popped again.

Roman, slightly frustrated, said, "Faye, it popped up again. How do we get it down?"

Suzie Germaine, our hairdresser, rushed in, intent on saving the day. Out of her bag of many tricks, she pulled out an aerosol can and blitzed the hair until it laid down obediently.

I yelled, "Roll camera," and right at that moment, that damn hair shot straight up again.

Roman, beginning to lose his patience, said, "I don't understand why this one hair won't stay down. Can we cut the hair?"

Faye, a bit insulted, said, "No, you're not cutting a hair on my head, Roman."

They begin to argue, with Roman volleying back, "Faye, you have four-hundred-seventy-thousand hair follicles. One hair isn't going to make a difference. Please. Let's cut the hair and get on with the shot."

Instead, Faye called Suzie back in, they did some more spraying, patting, matting, and fixing, and finally, the hair went down.

I rolled the camera and finally Roman said, "Action!"

Jack had the first line and as Faye was ready to respond, the hair, like an indolent child refusing to obey, shot up again. But Roman did not react or let Faye know the hair was up again. Instead, he snuck around her back where she couldn't see him...but we could watch in the camera. He deftly raised his hand, and before she knew he was there, he yanked the offending hair straight out of her head. She hurled every imaginable curse at him and then stormed off the set.

I called Bob Evans and told him what happened, curious what he wanted me to do.

He said, "What I want you to do is fix it."

Since it was now up to me to mend the relationship between Faye and Roman, I called Faye's agent, Joel Dean, and eventually, we were able to arrange a meeting where Roman apologized. Our talented costume designer, Anthea Sylbert, put a hat on Faye to make sure there would be no other wild hairs.

In the end, *Chinatown* was nominated for eleven Oscars and became one of the most iconic films of all time.

★ ★ ★

From the time I was a little kid, our family would never miss watching the Oscars. We'd probably seen all of the movies nominated for the big awards, so we'd have a betting pool where each of us would pick our winners. We didn't know much about the private lives of celebrities back then. This was way before *Entertainment Tonight, People* magazine, and the internet, so getting to see celebs live on the Oscars broadcast was really exciting.

The Academy Awards show is the gala to end all galas. In 1971 my father was asked to produce the Oscars, which of course was an enormous honor for him, not to mention a thrill for me because I'd get to be behind the scenes for some of it, and I'd be able to attend the show as well.

His first show was so successful that they asked him to produce it again. And again. And again. I'd go every year, and some years, if I wasn't shooting, I had the privilege of helping during preproduction. It's never stopped being a thrill for me. I was lucky enough to be there solely because my father was the producer, and for that, I was unequivocally grateful.

At the same time, I also felt that by now I had carved out and earned a place of my own by the good work I was doing. While I was visiting my father during rehearsals, he'd introduce me to his colleagues. After meeting me, every single one of them would say a version of what they'd been saying my entire life: what a wonderful man my father was, how much they loved my father, and eventually, "Are you in the business too?" It was an innocent question, but one that had the effect of reaffirming my conviction that no matter what I achieved in my own career, those achievements would forever be obscured by my father's.

It's hard to describe the extent to which those encounters always managed to take the wind out of my sails.

The year *Chinatown* was nominated, my dad was producing the show again. Thanks to him, Rita and I had great seats right behind Jack Nicholson, who was nominated for best actor along with Al Pacino for *Godfather II.* The best actor award is given out near the end of the show, but up until now our only win was Robert Towne's well-deserved best original screenplay award. *Godfather II* was cleaning up.

There was great suspense in the room when Glenda Jackson was about to announce the Best Actor award. Would it be Jack or Al? A huge upset occurred when Art Carney won for his role in *Harry and Tonto*. I leaned forward and whispered to Jack, "Aww, I'm so sorry." He turned to me and said, "That's okay, Bullhorn. I'm a shoo-in next year for *Cuckoo's Nest*."

20

After *Chinatown* I was hired to do *Once Is Not Enough*, a film that was integral to my relationship with my father because he was the producer, and I was asked to be both the AD and the production manager, a position I'd never held before. That meant I was going to be responsible not only for running the set as the AD, but also for managing all aspects of the production. It also meant there would be no middleman working between me and my dad.

It was a complex shoot with locations in LA, New York, Spain, and Switzerland. Some kind soul reassured me that if you have a great transportation captain, production coordinator, and unit managers in each one of the cities you'll be in, you'll be able to do your job. I followed this sage advice and ended up having a great experience.

I had been on sets watching my father produce movies for more than twenty years, but this was the first time I would have this much responsibility as part of his crew. The stakes felt high. I had so many questions: How were we going to interact with each other? Would this be my chance to really get close to him? I wondered if we'd share a drink at the end of the day and talk about life like I'd done with so many other producers. The simple answer turned out to be: no. No, we didn't interact except professionally; no, we didn't get any closer; and no, we never shared a drink at the end of the day. I followed his lead, which turned out to convey the message that our relationship was to remain strictly business. When the movie ended, I felt proud of the work I had done, and I knew on some level my father was proud of me too. I had set out to show him and the rest of the crew that I was more than my father's son and namesake. I wanted to prove that I was up to the task professionally, and I think I did that, even though the one disappointment was that the intimacy I hoped we could have didn't happen.

The next movie was *The Drowning Pool,* where I was the first AD to Stuart Rosenberg, with whom I'd done several movies. This would turn out to be the fourth and last film on which I'd work with Gordon Willis.

Stu told me, "We're gonna move you up. You're gonna be the associate producer *and* my first."

That was an exciting prospect for me for all kinds of reasons, not the least of which was that I'd be making a little more money.

The designer was a friend with whom I'd worked many times, Paul Sylbert, Dick Sylbert's twin brother. They were the two most talented production designers I ever worked with. Paul and I went down to Louisiana to scout for locations where I tasted boudin for the first time in my life.

The movie starred Paul Newman, Joanne Woodward, Anthony Franciosa, and Melanie Griffith. Melanie, who was sixteen at the time, made me promise that if her mom, Tippi Hedren, came down, I was sworn to secrecy about her new boyfriend, Don Johnson. Sorry, Tippi, I kept my promise.

I had worked with Paul Newman once before. He was a gem of a human being, and he loved playing practical jokes on people he was close to. His brother Arthur was our production manager. Arthur was bald and no matter the temperature, he always wore a hat. One day we were shooting at this antebellum mansion, and somehow Paul had managed to steal his brother's hat. Arthur was looking everywhere for it. Paul and his stunt double, Jim Arnett, were upstairs on the house's balcony.

Paul yelled down to his brother, "Hey, Arthur, what's the matter? You look upset."

"I can't find my hat," he yelled back up.

"Your hat?" says Paul, "Oh, I've got your hat right here."

And on that note, he tossed it high up into the air, skeet-style, whereupon Jim Arnett, shotgun in hand, shot the hat right out of the sky. What was formerly known as Arthur's hat floated down in a million pieces.

Throughout my career I've often been riveted by the performances given by some especially great actors the moment the camera rolls. Paul Newman and his wife, Joanne Woodward, were two of the best.

21

My father got ill in 1974 while I was prepping *The Drowning Pool*. He wasn't able to keep food down and started losing weight. I would only find out later that his symptoms had begun months earlier, but he and my mother had kept this information hidden.

He went to every specialist in Los Angeles, but no one was able to diagnose what it was. Finally, someone suggested he call the Mayo Clinic. When he did, he was told it would be six months before he could come in. He decided to call Ted Mann, of Mann Theaters, since he was from Minnesota. Thankfully, Ted got him into Mayo within the week.

My dad had had an ulcer operation in 1954, during which they partially cut the vagus nerve, which is responsible for the sphincter muscles in the esophagus. Over the years the muscle had atrophied so that by now nothing was opening and/or closing in order to squeeze the food down. They were going to have to perform an operation that had only been done a handful of times in the one-hundred-year history of the clinic, so needless to say we were all terrified, most of all, my father.

It was only when my mother told me he needed surgery that I realized the gravity of his situation. I was surprised at how hard it hit me. As far as I was concerned, my dad was a superhero. Even though I was an adult by now, the little boy in me was not prepared for facing the fact his dad was mortal. Besides, at twenty-eight I had never had to confront the possibility of losing anyone close to me before.

I thought, my God, I could actually lose him. The impact of that awareness stunned me, but as I had learned so well to do in my family, I stomped on my feelings and stepped into producing my father's operation instead.

I flew to Rochester, Minnesota, and met my sister, Melinda, who'd flown in from New York. We went in together to see our father before the operation. My mother, his shield, was with him when we walked in.

"Hey, how...how ya doin?" he asked, with a glaring superficial lightness that belied the gravity of his situation. His hands lifted in a one-two punch move that was accompanied by a "Ba da bing" as we approached, an easy way to fend off any incoming affection.

Melinda and I took our cue and met him in exactly that place and kept our end of the conversation light. When it was time for him to head to the operating room, my mother and sister remained in the room, but I wanted to stay with him, so I walked him down the hall on his gurney, each of us loyal to the silence between us.

We stopped outside the operating room doors, where I was not allowed to pass. To say that I was shocked when my father grabbed my forearm before we had to separate is an understatement of epic proportion. Other than shaking his hand, this was the only time I remembered feeling my father's touch. I froze, aware that something momentous was happening, and I was as terrified of it as I was hungry for it. I had no idea of knowing whether it would end at this physical gesture alone or if he would offer more.

Holding my arm, my father looked at me, really looked at me, straight in the eyes, and I held myself there in his gaze despite the urgency I felt to turn away from this alien paternal intimacy for which I had yearned my entire life.

He said earnestly, "If I don't come out of this, Howie, take care of your mother and sister."

I wasn't prepared for him to share with me his recognition that he could die. I wasn't prepared for the bare intimacy of that acknowledgment. As if it wasn't enough to grapple with the idea of being in the world without my father, he had added the reality of the responsibility he was handing to me, rendering me unable to say anything other than an emotionless "Of course."

To our great relief, the operation was successful and my dad fully recovered.

But I had been touched now—both literally and figuratively—and in that touch and the accompanying penetrating gaze, I had gotten a brief glimpse of the charge and the depth of love that can exist between a father and a son when they risk really looking at each other.

Even though my father and I never revisited that moment, at that instant, I felt what I had missed, and I knew what I wanted for and with my own children.

22

About that time I was getting the itch to move from being an AD to an executive producer. Having two kids, a wife, and a mortgage, I knew I couldn't stop everything to start developing material, because as a full creative producer you don't get paid until a movie gets going. I couldn't afford that. But I could work with a top director as an executive producer and AD. Not only would it move me up the chain, but it would give me more responsibility and more creative input than an AD had.

In films, the executive producer credit is given for several different functions. It could be given to someone who has put up part or all of the money to finance a movie. In the late '70s and early '80s, the executive producer credit started going to the top, experienced production managers. Often during the making of a film, producers don't have the time to sit on set every day making sure (from a production and a creative standpoint) that the vision for the movie is being carried out. When that happened, an executive producer (line producer) would become the day-to-day set person.

More and more producers were developing and packaging movies and letting others oversee the set. Although they watched dailies, kept in communication with the director and executive producer, they also kept an eye on the budget. It was the executive producer who worked on the set day-to-day, and that's what I wanted to do.

I felt I was uniquely qualified to perform any one of those producer functions, but I didn't want to be limited to just being the on-set executive producer. Every creative decision is a financial one, and every financial decision is a creative one, and I felt I was ready to do both. During my years of being an assistant director, my job was never defined by just doing the work of an AD. I was constantly in script discussions and any creative meetings with the director and the rest of his team. Since I was used to bridging the gap, I wanted to be both a creative and a line producer.

I figured that having my own agent would give me more access to producing jobs that were coming down the pike. I started to call around and set up some appointments for myself.

The agents saw me, told me how much they loved my dad, said they'd think about representing me, and promised to call me back. And then they never did.

By now I was used to being the disappointment when the person meeting or interviewing me really wanted to meet my father, Howard W. Koch, instead of me, the junior.

But I persevered and, eventually, found my way to an agent named Evarts Ziegler. He had a small, elite literary agency, Ziegler/Ross, with his partner, Hal Ross. Ziegler represented Sydney Pollack, which, as I think about it now, was probably how I got the meeting. I sat down with him, told him what I wanted to do and what my history was. I was conditioned by then to expect that when an agent said "I'll get back to you," it was code for "You'll never hear from me again." But to my surprise, after a couple of days, he actually did call me back.

"I've talked to a lot of people, and you have a good reputation and seem to know what you're doing. Come on back in, we want to represent you."

I was over the moon—this man represented William Goldman, Terry Malick, and my friend Jim Bridges. And now me.

When I came in to sign, he introduced me to a new agent named Steve Roth who had just started with Ziggy and would be my everyday go-to guy. Steve was around my age, and we hit it off.

The next morning Ziggy called me and said, "Come to the office right away and pick up a script. You're going to meet Mike Nichols at a bungalow at the Beverly Hills Hotel at four p.m."

I sprinted down, then went home to read *Bogart Slept Here* by Neil Simon. Having worked on *The Odd Couple* and *Barefoot in the Park,* I certainly knew Neil. Mike Nichols knew about me through his production designer Dick Sylbert, and he knew Roman, so my coming aboard the project must have made everybody comfortable because the next day Ziggy called to tell me I had the job. I would be the executive producer and the AD.

Anthea Sylbert, the costume designer I had worked with on *Chinatown* (as well as *Rosemary's Baby* and *Bad Company*), had been married to Dick's twin brother, Paul. We were social friends as well, so I was glad to see she was going to be the production designer and costume designer. I brought all the other people I'd been working with, including Dick Bruno, a costumer who had worked with Anthea and me in the past.

Bob Surtees, a great cameraman, came on and my buddy Jimmy Thornsbury was set to handle transportation. When you put a crew together, you're making a new family—it's not your primary family, but it is very close to one, at least for a time. It makes sense when you think about being on a set together from seven in the morning until eight or nine at night. When you're not working, you sit around and talk. You get to know one another intimately. When I put the crew together for *Bogart Slept Here,* I did it knowing I was putting together my movie family.

John Calley and Frank Wells, the heads of Warner Bros. at the time, said, "Mike isn't good at prep so we hope you can get him more prepared than usual."

I had learned how to do that well from Gordon Willis and Hank Moonjean, so I jumped in and somehow got Mike to hire every actor before we started shooting. Every set was built and decorated; all the costumes were agreed to, made, and paid for. All the locations were set up, so we knew exactly where we were going to shoot. This was my first producing job, and I wasn't going to leave one stone unturned. Mike Nichols was definitely prepared to make this movie.

Two weeks before shooting, we were going to have a script read-through on the stage at Warner Bros. We had a great cast, with Robert De Niro, Marsha Mason, Tony Lo Bianco, Sam Elliott, and Linda Lavin. Everyone there was excited, not just the cast but Mike Nichols, Neil Simon, Ray Stark, and John Calley. We started the reading, and there was a little bit of laughter because Neil Simon's words were just so damn funny.

De Niro started to speak, and he was basically reading the words, not acting. In a read-through that's okay but it began to seem as though he didn't understand the meter of a Neil Simon script.

A couple of looks were exchanged—the kind you know mean "Uh-oh, what's this?"—but those were eased by others that seemed to understand this was his first day, that he was just getting started. I don't think De Niro had a clue that this was going on around him.

With a little more reading it became obvious that De Niro, the hottest star in Hollywood, just couldn't find his groove. He had done *Bang the Drum Slowly, Mean Streets,* and *Godfather II,* none of which were exactly soda-coming-out-your-nose funny.

Everybody knew De Niro was the new Marlon Brando. He had just finished shooting *Taxi Driver,* and it was increasingly evident to us that he had yet to shed the character of Travis Bickle for this new role.

In our movie, De Niro's character was an off-off-Broadway actor who gets a screen test, then a callback, and then the job, ultimately bringing his family out to Hollywood. It's based on the story of how Dustin Hoffman got hired to star in *The Graduate.*

The first two weeks during rehearsal, De Niro was not doing well, which got Mike feeling insecure because he had a movie about to come out called *The Fortune,* with Jack and Warren, and he knew it wasn't his best work. Mike began to think that maybe he just wasn't funny anymore. That wasn't true, but still, he worried.

We started shooting and each new day was worse than the one before it. I was trying to think positively, but De Niro was playing it in a way that was—shall we say—not remotely evocative of mirth.

On day seven of filming, the scene involved De Niro and Marsha Mason coming to Hollywood after he'd gotten the job. They're supposed to drive up in a yellow cab to a yellow house that the studio had rented for them. The yellow house had yellow flowers in the front and a little yellow brick path. Can you picture it? When you opened the yellow door, there were yellow rugs, yellow walls, yellow furniture. We'd even put yellow water in the swimming pool.

We were ready to begin the first rehearsal of the day. The plan was that Marsha and Bob would go up to the front door—the act of which was funny in itself because the art direction was so utterly over the top as to be ridiculous. Ridiculously yellow.

Marsha's first line was "Gee, it's very yellow."

De Niro's line was "Yeah, it is yellow. Don't you like yellow?"

And her reply was "Yes, I like yellow. I just never thought anybody would use it all up. Bobby, who found this place?"

He says, "Some lady from the studio. She was sick," to which Marsha was to reply, "Probably jaundice."

We'd get the laugh and then we're out of the scene.

We did the first rehearsal, we came up to the door, and everyone was laughing, and Marsha said brightly, "Gee, it's very yellow."

De Niro hemmed and hawed until he replied darkly, "Yeah...oooh, yeah, it is yellow. Do you, do you like yellow?"

She said sweetly, "Oh, yes, I like yellow. I just never thought anybody would use it all up. Bobby, who found this place?"

Instead of his line, De Niro looked at Nichols and asked in true method acting style, "Do I know this woman from the studio, Mike?"

Mike, slightly annoyed, said, "I don't know Bobby, why?"

"Well, how do I know she's sick?" he implored, clearly needing to know before he could go on.

Nichols, bad mood rising, said, "Bobby, look at this place! Who would rent a house like this to anybody? It's horrible!"

Unrelentingly curious and determined to plumb the depths of his motivation, De Niro asked, "Well, could I say she's probably sick?"

Through his clenched teeth, Nichols said, "No, Bobby. Because then Marsha's line, 'Probably jaundice,' doesn't work."

Seeing the smoke wafting out of Mike's ears, I said, "You know what—why don't we lay the dolly track while Bobby and Marsha go to makeup?" The moment they all left, Nichols turned to me and fumed, "I will not work another minute with this guy. I'm firing him."

I'm thinking, are you kidding me? You're going to fire Robert De Niro? Seven days into shooting? On my first producing gig? This can't be!

Turns out, it could be. We went to the editing room that morning with John Calley to show him the six days of our work and discuss Mike's feelings. Calley and Nichols had been best friends for years, so he said to Mike, "Okay, if you want to fire him, fire him, and we'll find somebody else."

Mike Nichols, appeased, fired Robert De Niro that day, and for two weeks we tried to recast the movie. When nobody wanted to replace De Niro, Calley and Mike and I had a meeting the morning of September 19, 1975.

While the entire crew waited on the stage, Calley said to Mike and me, "We're going to abandon the film. Figure out how you can cut our losses."

I had spent a lot of Warner Bros. money thoroughly prepping Mike. So along with the giant failure of losing my first producing gig, that Friday was not just a very black one, but an extremely expensive one for the studio.

I hated going to the stage that day to tell the whole crew we were shutting down the movie. "You have three days to wrap up," I would say to this one, or "I'm sorry but today's your last day" to another.

Sick to my stomach from the day's events, I drove home to tell Rita the bad news. She listened to me without saying a word. When I was finished telling her the whole story, she floored me by telling me she wanted a divorce.

Because *Bogart Slept Here* was my first real producing job, I had spent all my time on it, neglecting my home life. Because I did, I had no idea how unhappy Rita was.

The only thing I can think of by way of understanding the timing of her decision was that she had made up her mind and must have needed to say it right away in order not to back down.

I gathered a few things and zombie-walked out the door to go stay at a buddy's apartment. I lived in a fetal position for days contemplating this new low of lows.

I still couldn't eat or sleep and stayed fairly catatonic for a few days while trying to absorb the hit of having lost my family and my first producing job in the same day.

Two years after *Bogart Slept Here* fell apart, Neil Simon reworked it into *The Goodbye Girl*. It received five Oscar nominations, including best picture. Richard Dreyfuss won the Oscar for best actor. Herb Ross directed it.

★ ★ ★

A few weeks into my depression, I was rescued by the ringing of the telephone. I doubted I had the energy to say hello, but I'm a Koch, so I picked it up.

The person on the other end filled in the emptiness with a drawn out and very deep, "Uhhh...hello...Howard."

"Oh, hi, Bob," I answered listlessly.

"Uhhh, how'd you know it was me?"

"I recognized your voice."

Bob was Bob Evans, well known for his characteristic deep voice.

"How ya doin'?" he asked.

"Not very well. How about you?"

"I'm shooting *Marathon Man*."

"Yeah? How's it going?"

"Uhhh, we've been shooting ten days. We're ten days behind."

When I asked him what was the problem, he answered with a quick, "I don't know. Why do you think I'm calling you?"

I perked up a bit to ask, "Where are you shooting?"

"Mount Kisco, about an hour outside of New York City," he said.

"Is that where you are now?"

He paused a beat before saying, "No, I'm at the Carlyle with a blonde."

That was Bob.

We made the deal right then on the phone, and I took the red-eye that night, read the script on the plane, and landed at five-thirty in the morning at JFK. I was driven to the Ramada Inn in Mount Kisco. I was to be the first AD, Bob's eyes and ears. He was producing the movie, and my job was to try and put it back on track. I took a quick shower and jumped in the car with John Schlesinger, the director, and Conrad Hall, the cinematographer, both Academy Award winners.

We drove up to Pound Ridge where the scene was going to take place. In the scene, Dustin Hoffman and Marthe Keller drive up to a white house on a hill. It had a long, long driveway. Upon arrival at the house, they had a short dialogue scene to play.

I felt the need to stay quiet and not jump in like I normally do. I just wanted to watch for a day so that I could get my bearings.

When we arrived and got out of the car, Schlesinger turned to Connie and, in his upper-crust English accent that made you want to clear your throat and stand up straighter, said, "Connie, how about a thirty-five mill and we'll see the car in the distance? As the car comes up the long driveway, we'll pan over, and there'll be the house, and then we'll cut."

It wasn't a question as much of a thinking-out-loud statement.

Connie said, "Well, that's okay, John, but what about a hundred mill? We get back a little farther and a little tighter on the car and as we pan over, the house will kind of be out of focus in the foreground. It would make a better cut."

John and Connie went back and forth in this manner, each with a different idea of how to do the drive-up.

It was beginning to feel more like a preproduction meeting than a shooting day.

Dustin walked up and said, "Oh, hi, Howard. I heard you were coming. It's totally screwed up here. I hope you can help."

He turned to John and said, "I've got to talk to you."

I heard a bit of John's frustration as he replied, "What is it, Dustin?"

"Well I've got a problem with today's scene," he said, "I can't do the scene today. The dialogue just doesn't work."

John said, "I'll be with you in a minute, Dustin," whereupon he turned to me and said under his breath, "Oh, gawd, what am I gonna do?"

More planning ensued, more time was wasted, and more silence came from me.

Eventually John threw up his hands and said to Connie, "I don't know what we should do. I've got to go talk to Dustin!"

We'd been there since a quarter past seven in the morning. It was now nine thirty and not one damn thing had been accomplished. No wonder we were ten days behind. At this rate, the movie would never get made. I was twenty-nine years old and was now faced with three Academy Award winners who couldn't seem to make any decisions.

John had been in Dustin's trailer for a long time while the crew stood around with nothing to do except wait to *begin* a whole day's shooting. At some point, I'd finally had enough. I knocked on the door of Dustin's trailer.

When John answered it, I said, "I've got to talk to you. And I brought Connie with me too."

He said, "I'm talking to Dustin right now," at which point the words "No, I need to talk to you now" flew out of my mouth and hit him straight on.

I walked into the trailer and, as a recent graduate of the Gordon Willis school of film prep, said with assurance, "John, you're the director. You have to know exactly what you want to shoot every day.

That's your job. You have to know what shots you want and how you're going to shoot them." Silence.

Pulling another arrow out of my quiver, I set my sights on Connie this time. "And Connie, you have every right to make a suggestion. One suggestion. And John, between what you decided you wanted to do when you were prepping and Connie's one suggestion, we will make a decision, and that will be the shot."

You could have heard a feather land on the floor. Or at least it was quiet enough so that we all heard Dustin from the opposite end of his trailer when he asked, "What does all this have to do with me?"

At that moment the storm that had been brewing inside of me for weeks gathered itself and slammed into the room tornado-style.

I turned to him and raged, "This has everything to do with you, Dustin! You have every right to have a problem with a scene"—at which point a smile began to form on his face until I went on—"a *week* ahead of time. You have *NO* right on the day of shooting to decide you don't like the scene. We're filming today's scene as it's written. I will get William Goldman [the author and screenwriter] up here tonight and you, he, and John will go over the next few days, then the next week after that. We're going to stay a week ahead of time, so we don't lose any more days."

I was finished and spent. Had I really just said all that? I had, and because I stood my professional ground, we got the day's work done, and we only lost one more day in the next seventy-five days of shooting.

A lot of personal and professional circumstances converged at that moment that compelled me to stand up to those three icons of our business. Once I did, I felt confident I knew what I was talking about, and that was a game changer for me. A lot of professional people know what they're talking about. Their instincts are good, but they're afraid to stand up and express themselves to the people with the power. Finding my voice in that particular moment changed my career and began the healing process I so badly needed.

Sir Laurence Olivier was going to play Szell, who, in his adept hands, entered the pantheon of iconic Hollywood film villains. Sir Laurence arrived to do his work about three weeks after we'd begun filming. He hadn't been in a movie for several years because he had cancer and, as a result, was uninsurable. After all, if something happened to him and he couldn't continue, the movie would have to be re-cast, and all of Szell's scenes re-shot. Everyone in Hollywood knows no studio would hire an uninsurable actor. No studio, that is, except Paramount, because Bob Evans didn't care.

We were shooting at the Delacourt Clock in Central Park Zoo on the first day Sir Laurence was to work. He arrived promptly at nine o'clock in the morning with his makeup on and in wardrobe. You could see he was a bit stooped—a shadow of the man he used to be. To my eye, he didn't seem at all well and I wasn't so sure he was going to make it.

As he walked up toward the set, the prop man said to him respectfully, "Sir Laurence, which watch would you like to be wearing?" At the same time, the costumer approached with an equal amount of respect to ask, "May I put your coat on?" The makeup and hair people were starting to fuss over him, and then John Schlesinger approached and started talking to him about the scene. When Sir Laurence first came out, he was like a half-inflated balloon, but with each of these encounters, and as he started to work, that deflated balloon started to fill up and come back to life right before our eyes. And that was just day one!

He worked with us for about two more weeks in New York. Every day he got better and better, and his posture improved as we all witnessed him return to that regal, powerful man we had known him to be. He was doing what he loved once again and that restored him.

When we came back to L.A., we started shooting on the stages. I remember him coming to me one day and asking, "My boy, what are you doing tonight after we finish shooting?"

"I'm probably going home, I'm tired," I said. "What are you doing?" When he said, "I'm going to R.J. and Natalie's house (meaning Robert

Wagner and Natalie Wood); they're having a dinner party for me," his pride was palpable.

A lot of people in L.A. started inviting him out. He was in his element and it showed. I think he made five movies in a row after that before he became too sick to work anymore. It was very exciting and life-affirming to watch his transition.

One day during filming, we had a scene to do on Forty-Seventh Street between Fifth and Sixth Avenues in New York City—the diamond district. The block on both sides of the street is filled with retail and wholesale jewelry dealers, most of whom are Hasidic Jews with black hats and robes, long beards, and side locks called *payot*.

In the scene, Sir Laurence Olivier, as Szell, is walking down the street when a Jewish crone suddenly recognizes him as the Nazi she remembers, and begins to yell, increasingly louder and more vehemently, "Der Weisse Engel! Der Weisse Engel!"

We had about one hundred background actors, all dressed as Hasidic Jews, surrounding the old lady. We had a camera hidden in the window of a van, another one in a storefront, and one more on a roof looking down on the crowd. When the crone yelled, "Der Weisse Engel," it wasn't just our one hundred background actors who stopped and stared at Szell; everyone on the street froze at the eerie proclamation that the Nazi angel of death was walking among them.

It was a spine-chilling moment I will never forget.

★ ★ ★

The story of what happened on *Marathon Man* between Dustin and Sir Laurence has by now become Hollywood lore, but since I witnessed it, I can attest to its veracity.

Dustin's character was in a lot of pain after having his teeth drilled. He was suffering horribly, couldn't sleep, and was taking a lot of pain medication. Dustin was taking occasional sips from a Styrofoam cup he was holding that might have been filled with whiskey for all I know. He was using what's called "method acting" for the scene.

Let's just say that Dustin was being very emotive and expressive when we were shooting the climactic scene of the film in the Central Park Waterworks. He kept flubbing his lines, flubbing his lines, and flubbing his lines some more, until we were all becoming more and more frustrated. As we were getting ready for the umpteenth take, Sir Laurence, who was clearly tired of it at this point, looked at Dustin and said, "Dustin, why don't you just try acting?"

A hush fell over the whole set. Dustin, startled by the remark, looked at Sir Laurence, took a breath, put down his Styrofoam cup, and delivered his lines perfectly.

★ ★ ★

When we were back in LA and finishing up, I got a call from Steven Spielberg. The man himself called me on the phone and said, "Hi, this is Steven. I want to come talk to you about doing a movie with me. Would you mind?"

Would I mind? No!

For good—as well as for bad—I'm the guy about whom you never have to wonder what he's thinking. I always lose at poker. I wear it all on my sleeve, so I said, "Are you kidding me? Sure, come over!"

Steven Spielberg actually came over at lunchtime to meet me. I could hardly believe it when I found myself on my lunch break sitting at one of the catering tables talking to him about his next film. He'd heard about me and asked if I would read the script. If I liked it, he said he'd want me to come work with him on it and be one of the producers. He had some creative producers on board, but none of them were production savvy.

Of course, I said yes. I read it that night when I got home from work, and I was beside myself with excitement. I called Steven the next day and told him, "I think it's phenomenal. I'd love to work on it with you." We talked all the way through the script, and just before getting off the phone he said, "Great, let me go talk to the people at Columbia Pictures."

I spent a couple of days waiting for that call. When it finally came, he said, "I'm sorry, Howard. I've got two producers on the film, and they won't let me add anybody else." Yes, even Steven Spielberg, at that time in his career, had to get approvals from the studio.

And that's the story of how I never got to be part of *Close Encounters of the Third Kind*.

You win some, you lose some, and some are rained out.

23

I was the first of all my friends to get married. I was the first to be a father. And now I was the first to get divorced and stumble my way through that painful passage. I don't think it can be overstated how hard that is.

I knew I wanted Billy (who was almost six) and Emily (nearly three) with me on the weekends. Emily was not a happy kid—and who could blame her, she was so young when Rita and I split up. Billy was better equipped to handle the change with his go-with-the-flow, everyone's-invited personality that he seemed born with.

One of the saddest memories I have is of dropping my kids off on Sunday evenings. I will always be haunted by the grief that overcame me as I watched them run back into the house to be with their mom.

One of the ways I got a chance to spend more time with my kids was to coach Billy's baseball teams and attend Emily's soccer games. I ducked out of work during the week every chance I got.

I continued my search for "real" love, a truly enduring one like my parents had. Out of necessity that led to a lot of personal research, which of course meant dating a lot of women and sometimes disappointing a lot of people because of it, most regrettably my kids.

In 1976, I was living in an apartment off Sunset, dating no one in particular, and executive producing *The Other Side of Midnight*, based on a best-selling book by Sidney Sheldon.

Our budget was $9 million. Word came down from the head of the studio, Alan Ladd, Jr., that they weren't going to make it unless we cut a million dollars. The producer called me into his office and basically told me, "Go figure it out."

My first thought was to discuss it with our brilliant production designer, John DeCuir. He was a three-time Oscar winner for *The King and I, Cleopatra,* and *Hello, Dolly!* The first time we met, before we could talk about the business at hand or even any of his own classic movies, he—like so many before him—regaled me with stories about his experience with my dad while they were making *On a Clear Day You Can See Forever.*

Eventually, John and I did put our heads together and came up with an idea of how to save that million dollars.

Instead of going to Greece as planned, we discussed going to Palos Verdes and building some foreground pieces made to look like the Isle of Crete. With that and a couple of other large trims, we'd save a million and would now have our $8 million budget.

When I told our producer, he looked at me with fire in his eyes and ushered me out the door insisting, "That's the worst fucking idea I've ever heard."

It's fair to say that was a severe blow to my professional confidence.

Later that afternoon I got a call from the head of physical production at Fox, Ray Gosnell, Jr., telling me to come to his office to hear the good news. Turns out, the producer (of ripping me a new one fame) had gone to Alan Ladd to share his idea of how to cut a million out of the budget.

If you haven't already guessed, he suggested we shoot Palos Verdes for Greece, make a few other cuts, and poof! we're down to eight million. Everyone loved "his" idea, and suddenly we were back in business.

Just goes to show you that credit doesn't always land in the right place. But at least we had a movie to make.

* * *

While I was prepping the movie, a mutual friend set me up on a blind date. Marcia was funny and pretty and had a vulnerability that I found myself drawn to. We had a lot in common: we liked the same music and the same movies, and we were compatible intellectually.

I thought she was great with Billy and Emily, and she was sympathetic, listening intently when I told her I didn't feel I'd had the chance in my first marriage to have the kind of relationship I wanted with my kids. We both wanted a child, and I believed it would be different with Marcia.

* * *

When I finished *The Other Side of Midnight*, I got a call from Warren Beatty. I'd worked with Warren on *The Parallax View*, and he had asked me to do *Shampoo*, but unfortunately, I had been unavailable. Warren told me to meet him at the Hideaway, the bar at the Beverly Wilshire Hotel. At that time, he was living in the penthouse of the hotel while building his dream home. We met in a tiny dark corner of The Hideaway bar, and we talked about the movie he wanted to make called *Heaven Can Wait*.

Talking is a funny word for an exchange with Warren, because he keeps everything very close to his vest. He gives just enough information to elicit a response so that he can gauge it against what only he knows he's looking for. It's a test disguised as a conversation, containing mostly questions (his) and answers (yours).

Heaven Can Wait was to be a remake of a movie I was familiar with, called *Here Comes Mr. Jordan*. Warren went fishing: "How would you organize and shoot a sequence that is supposed to be the Super Bowl?"

Our meeting ended soon after I told him how I imagined it might work.

A few days later, I had a deal with Paramount to be both executive producer and Warren's AD on the film. Warren was going to star and direct for the first time.

It was during the long prep of *Heaven Can Wait* that Marcia and I got married one afternoon at my parents' house. It was a small wedding with a bigger evening reception at Marcia's parents' house. I was excited to be back on the trajectory of creating a marriage like the one my parents had.

24

Warren Beatty hired Buck Henry to be his codirector. As his executive producer and assistant director, he leaned on me quite a bit, as much as Warren can lean on anybody. I enjoyed the responsibility I carried.

The Los Angeles Rams football team is a major component of the film, and the Rams winning the Super Bowl was a critical scene at the end of the film. We were able to get permission from the National Football League, as well as the owners of the Rams and the Pittsburgh Steelers, who would be the opposing team in our fictitious Super Bowl. Our plan was to shoot the critical scene of Warren scoring the winning touchdown during the fourteen-minute halftime of a real Rams-Steelers exhibition game at the Coliseum.

We hired recently retired football players who were well known to Los Angeles fans to represent the two teams, with Warren playing quarterback for the Rams. We got real NFL referees and all the other important sideline officials, as well as background actors to play the rest of the teams. We had six cameras and would shoot both before, during, and after the game.

I had been talking to Jack Teele, the former general manager of the Rams, about it. He kept telling me, "Now, you know, we always have a great halftime show so you gotta make sure that our customers aren't disappointed."

I kept assuring him it would be a great show. Every time I talked to Jack during the weeks leading up, he'd remind me, "Make sure you got a good show!"

When the day finally arrived, I ran into Jack, who nervously queried, again, "You got a good halftime show for me, right?"

"You bet I do," I insisted, hoping we could pull it off.

Our scene was based on the "Immaculate Reception," one of the most famous plays in the history of football. It happened during a 1972 AFC divisional playoff game between the Oakland Raiders and the Steelers. With no time left on the clock, Terry Bradshaw, the quarterback, threw a pass. The ball hit an Oakland Raider's helmet and ricocheted right into the hands of Steelers running back Franco Harris, who ran forty-five yards for the winning touchdown.

In our film, Warren throws the ball, but instead of it ricocheting into the running back's hands, it ricochets back into Warren's hands, and he runs fifty yards for the victory.

We wanted to start close on Warren as they broke the huddle so that even though he was wearing a helmet, you could clearly see it was Warren Beatty coming up to the line of scrimmage.

When it was halftime and we were ready to go, the real Rams ran off the field, whereupon all of the retired Rams, the old football players, and the production crew, ran onto the field. As planned, my friend Paul Picerni, who was the public address announcer at that time, said over the loudspeakers, "Don't go away, fans, because tonight at halftime, the Rams are gonna win the Super Bowl!"

We started shooting our scene, and as we did, Paul started announcing to the crowd, "Hey, see number eighty-four over there on the right end for the Rams—that's Jack Snow!" or "There's Deacon Jones, and there's Merlin Olsen!"

All these great, retired Rams were actually running the plays for us. The fans got really into it, standing up, applauding, doing everything we'd hoped they'd do. They loved it! We got all that and even more in the fourteen limited minutes we had.

Warren—the perfectionist—was beside himself because as both star and director he didn't have time to come back between takes to look at the video playbacks. It required him to trust us, and just as introspection was not my strong suit, trust wasn't Warren's.

Billy Fraker (the DP) and I kept yelling, "Warren, do it again! Keep going!" and he'd run another fifty yards down the field. He was exhausted by the end, but we got great stuff, and Billy and I had a great laugh.

When I saw Jack Teele, I couldn't wait to ask him, "Did you have a good halftime for the Rams customers?"

To my surprise, he said, "It was awful!"

"Awful? What are you talking about?" I asked, incredulously. "The fans were cheering, having a great time. How is that awful?"

He said grimly, "Nobody went out to buy hotdogs. We had the worst concession sales we've ever had. That's what I mean by awful."

Sometimes you just can't win.

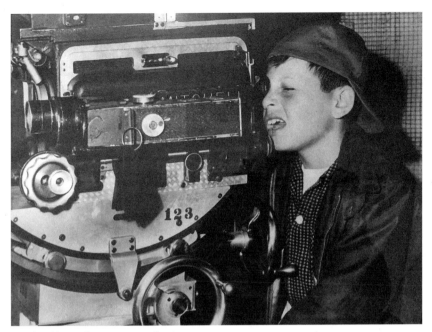

Loving filmmaking at an early age.

With Mamie Van Doren...SCHWINGGG!

My grandparents, Billy and Bea Koch, on the
boardwalk in Atlantic City.

With Redford on the set of *This Property Is Condemned*.

Natalie Wood...EXCELLENT! © Paramount Pictures Corp. All Rights Reserved.

On the set of *Barefoot in the Park* with Jane Fonda and Redford. © Paramount Pictures Corp. All Rights Reserved.

Jack Lemmon and Walter Matthau on the set of *The Odd Couple.*
© Paramount Pictures Corp. All Rights Reserved.

Mia Farrow on the set of *Rosemary's Baby.* © Paramount Pictures Corp.
All Rights Reserved.

A serious moment with Barbra on the set of *The Way We Were*. THE WAY
WE WERE © 1973, renewed 2001 Columbia Pictures Industries, Inc.
All Rights Reserved. Courtesy of Columbia Pictures.

On the set of *The Parallax View* with (left to right) Tom Overton, me,
Warren Beatty, Gordon Willis, and Alan Pakula. © Paramount Pictures Corp.
All Rights Reserved.

On location for *Chinatown* with Roman Polanski and Jack Nicholson.
© Paramount Pictures Corp. All Rights Reserved.

At the LA Coliseum filming *Heaven Can Wait* with Warren Beatty.
© Paramount Pictures Corp. All Rights Reserved.

At the climax of *Marathon Man* with Sir Laurence Olivier and John Schlesinger.
© Paramount Pictures Corp. All Rights Reserved.

25

Bob Towne was set to direct, for the first time in his career, his screenplay *Greystoke: The Legend of Tarzan*, for Warner Bros. When he asked if I would produce it for him, I jumped at the chance. I was going to be both the creative and the line producer. It was one of the most talked about scripts at the time, and I was honored to be a part of it.

Since I had been in Africa with Streisand in 1972, I felt my previous experience there would be useful to Bob.

Location scouting is one of the most fun things you can do on a movie. Not only is it intensely creative, but you get to learn about the culture and the people wherever you are. Typically, you end up meeting with the chamber of commerce, the mayor, the hardware store owner, police, fire, highway patrol. You go into churches and temples, all the while listening to stories about the places you're considering for your location. There's a big difference between the way you're treated by the locals when you're scouting and shooting, compared to being a tourist. You're invited in to know the different cultures.

Once again, we traveled to Kenya to scout, this time looking for somewhere Tarzan, king of the jungle, might live. Tarzan's jungle environment evokes rivers and a world teeming with flora—tall trees dripping with vines he can swing on—and fauna—screeching chimpanzees and other wild creatures roaming free.

One day, we headed out with our guide in a Land Rover. We, in this case, was me, Bob Towne, and John Box, a very proper and talented English production designer who'd won Oscars for *Doctor Zhivago, Lawrence of Arabia,* and *Oliver!* The man was not a lightweight. Since Warner Bros. was footing the bill, their London head of physical production, Paul Hitchcock, was also on the scout.

After a long day's scout, we returned to the Mount Kenya Safari Club and were told that Adnan Khashoggi, a Saudi arms dealer and one of the richest men in the world at that time, had recently purchased it. Knowing we were in Africa scouting locations, we were told Mr. Khashoggi wanted to meet with us because he was hoping we'd use his club as our home base. Mr. Khashoggi's front man suggested lunch at William Holden's game preserve the next day. Bill Holden loved Africa and, as part owner of the Mount Kenya Safari Club, had put together a game preserve right outside the gates of the club that held every imaginable species of African wildlife.

Saying no to the man who owned the place where we were staying was out of the question, so arrangements were made to meet with him the following day at noon.

There was only one structure on the preserve, a one-story, bunkerlike house for the game warden. Since there were no trees, both the land and the house were completely exposed to the sweltering African heat. It was a sight to behold Mount Kenya towering over this vast empty plain.

Despite the harsh environment, we were standing outside amid carved ice sculptures of African animals. Since we'd all assumed Mr. Khashoggi was inside the bunker house, we were entirely taken aback when we heard a helicopter approaching. It landed right in front of us and out from it stepped Mr. Khashoggi along with his beautiful girlfriend.

After the introductions were made, we moved to a semicircle of deck chairs, behind which a corral held two intimidating and angry looking cape buffalo.

Mr. Khashoggi explained, "For your predining pleasure, I have brought in the prima ballerina of belly dancing in all of Egypt, along with her orchestra."

Right on cue, out of that bunker house came twelve Egyptian musicians in black tuxedos followed by one belly dancer. It's fairly obvious to say that the last thing we would have expected on a blazing hot afternoon on the equator in the African sun would be twelve guys in tuxedoes and the *bum ba da bum dum, bum ba da bum bumming* of a belly dancer.

It was surreal, and we did everything we could to keep straight faces, a feat we achieved by not making eye contact with one another.

At some point during the performance, I turned around to look at the cape buffalo. They appeared as gobsmacked as we were at the extent to which humans will go to impress one another.

In the end, we were no longer attached to *Greystoke*. When they finally made it, Robert was so upset with the end result, he refused to put his name on it as the credited writer. The pseudonym he used for *Greystoke* was P. H. Vazak, the name of his beloved dog.

26

Up to this point I had been an executive producer on *Bogart Slept Here, The Other Side of Midnight, Heaven Can Wait,* and *The Frisco Kid.* While I was creatively involved in those films, mainly I was doing what today is known as line producing. I enjoyed my work immensely, but there were still producers who kicked off the whole shebang by finding the material and seeing it through all the way to the end. I wasn't that guy; I wanted to be, but I knew I wasn't a great self-starter. I believe it's as important to know your weaknesses as it is your strengths. Creating the idea for a movie was not one of my strengths, and I knew if I were going to be a full-fledged producer, I'd need a partner.

I asked my agent, Steve Roth, who had now moved from Ziegler to CAA, if he knew anyone looking for a partner who might be more of an idea guy than I was.

Steve immediately said, "You've got to meet Gene Kirkwood."

I didn't know Gene at all, so Steve set up a meeting for us. I went to Gene's house in Stone Canyon, and the first thing I noticed once inside was an Oscar sitting proudly on his mantel. I had no idea what he'd won it for, but I took it as a sign, a good omen.

We talked for a while about what we wanted to do in our lives and what kinds of movies we wanted to make. It seemed like we had a similar sensibility. Gene was a great salesman. He had a lot of energy, and I liked him immediately.

At some point toward the end of our visit, I looked back up at his mantel and said, "It must be great to have an Oscar."

"The only reason I have it is because of your dad."

Oh, my God, here it comes again. I braced myself.

"What do you mean?" I asked stumbling.

I don't think Gene noticed a shift in my equilibrium because he went straight into saying, "My old friend Sylvester Stallone and I were two out-of-work actors. We had so little money that we used to go to a bank on Sunset Boulevard, around the corner from the friend's apartment we were crashing, to get Danish they'd put out for their customers in the morning. That's the only way we were going to have breakfast.

"Sly had only been in a couple of films, including *The Lords of Flatbush*, but he'd written a script that was going around town. Paramount offered him one hundred and fifty thousand dollars for it, but I told him to turn it down."

"What?" I asked Gene incredulously. "You guys were broke, and you turned down 150 Gs?"

Gene said, "You bet. I told him, 'No way, you gotta be the lead. You gotta turn it down. We're gonna get it made, and you're gonna star in it. Just wait and see.'"

That was Gene: terminally positive.

He was able to get the script to Chartoff/Winkler, who had what's called a "put deal" at United Artists. That meant they could tell United Artists what movie to make with one caveat: it couldn't cost more than a million dollars. Chartoff/Winkler liked the movie enough that they used their put deal and then let Gene executive produce it. They got John Avildsen, who Gene knew, to direct it and Stallone to star. Of course, that film was *Rocky*.

Even though Gene was on the set the whole time and produced the movie in the truest sense of the word, Chartoff/Winkler had the put deal and were big producers, so they got the producer credit.

When the picture was nominated for an Oscar, Gene said, "Wow, we got a shot at winning an Oscar!"

Irwin and Bob set him straight by telling him, "Well, Gene, no. You're an executive producer. Only the producer is nominated for an Oscar."

Gene was crushed.

Rocky did win best picture. Both Chartoff and Winkler went up and accepted the award with Stallone, but not Gene.

As Gene was telling me the story, he reminded me that my dad was president of the Academy the year *Rocky* won.

"When your dad heard that I was really the guy who produced the movie, he very quietly had an Oscar with my name on it delivered to my house in a brown paper bag. That's how I got that Oscar up there on my mantel, Howard. Your dad is one class act."

"Yeah, he sure is," I agreed.

With Gene, however, something about this territory felt different. He might be the first person who didn't lead our meeting with an anecdote about how great my father was. I appreciated that, and I liked him, so I decided to give it a try and that day we formed Koch/Kirkwood Productions.

27

Marcia and I were compatible when it came to the life we envisioned for ourselves, and we were speeding ninety-five miles an hour toward it. We both wanted a child, and we couldn't have been more thrilled when in March 1979, our beautiful son, Robby (named after my old pal, Robbie Long), was born.

We moved to within a few blocks of Billy and Emily, so they could see their baby brother whenever they wanted. They adored him from the moment they met him at two days old. Billy, then nine, put a little rubber football into his crib and asked, "When do you think he's gonna be ready to play ball with me?"

"Me too!" Emily piped up, determined not to be left out. "When will he be able to play with me too?"

As thrilled as I was—and I was—it didn't take long to realize that the same challenge I had faced with Rita had begun to emerge with Marcia. Once she became a mother, Robby became the center of Marcia's universe.

That's when I realized it must be me. I just didn't know that relegating everyone except the baby to the back burner was natural for new mothers, a necessary part of motherhood and important for the baby's development.

You have to understand that unlike today, there were no books or talk shows explaining to men what to expect when the baby's born.

We all just winged it. When it dawned on me that this was natural behavior, I was comforted by the rationale that, like everything else, balance would eventually be restored and the pendulum would swing back because that too was important for the child's development.

Stronger men than I might have withstood the displacement, but I was not equipped to do so back then. I was young and needed to be seen, and I was still searching for my own sense of identity.

Gene and I were starting a new production company, and we were trying to get our first film, *The Idolmaker*, going while bringing in some much-needed money. I had a wife and new baby to support, as well as alimony and child support for my ex-wife and two older children.

As a line producer on film after film, I had a steady income. But nobody pays a creative producer to find material. Once you find a project, you have to develop the screenplay and then try to find someone who will finance it for you. No matter how well or how poorly all that is going, you're still not making any money at that point. What you are trying to do is to package it. You want to get a director and an actor or actress passionate enough to join up in trying to get it made. You want it to be as complete a package as possible.

If you're a gambler, you may know there's something called "the come line" at the crap table, where you put money down to see if certain numbers will "come." Gene and I were on that line waiting to see if any of our projects were going to get traction.

Once you do get traction or a financier—say, a studio—you might hire a writer who'll get many thousands of dollars up front to write the project. As a producer, the fee for development is today what it always has been, $25,000, half of which you get at the start of your development deal. Keep in mind that if you have a partner, like I did, that half is split, meaning you will get $6,250 for the year, or maybe even for two years if it takes that long to get your project going.

You get the other $12,500—which again you will split with your partner—either when the movie goes into production or turnaround. Turnaround means the studio decides not to make it, but if that's the case, you're allowed to start the process all over and try to find someone else who will. As I said, it's extremely stressful.

Our finances were in such a precarious place that we increasingly needed to tighten our belts. This was the moment in our marriage when I learned that belt-tightening was neither of our fortes. I began to lose more and more of what little authority and self-esteem I possessed. Although I didn't know it at the time, I began to give up. I wasn't mature enough to see the pattern in my own behavior. Had I been able to, I might have sought outside help.

I wasn't good at asking for help but I was good at work, so I just threw my energy into the new company. When Gene and I became partners, he'd already been working on an early draft of *The Idolmaker,* based on the true story of music manager Bob Marcucci. In the late '50s and early '60s, Bob discovered and managed both Frankie Avalon and Fabian. He was absolutely driven to turn these two young boys into American idols.

Gene had a relationship with the young actor Ray Sharkey. Ray had read an early draft, and we all thought he was the perfect guy to play the lead. Although neither Gene nor I thought *The Idolmaker* screenplay was great, we thought it had enough going for it to get a development deal somewhere. We sent it to David Field, who was running United Artists at the time. I had never met David before, but we went into his impressive office at the old Thalberg building, which is now owned by Sony Pictures. Gene, David, and I talked about the movie and what we each saw as its potential. David made a deal with us right then to develop the project. He and I really hit it off. He became and remains one of my closest friends.

While looking for a director, I got a call from Stephanie Brodie, an agent at CAA.

She said, "I'd like you to see a short film my client, a new young director named Taylor Hackford, made."

In those days you couldn't look up anyone on IMDb or see their work on YouTube, so Gene and I went into a projection room to watch the film, not knowing anything about it other than it was fifteen minutes long and was called *Teenage Father.*

Once we started watching it, we realized it was a documentary. It was so well done, but I couldn't understand how Taylor could have talked these kids and their parents into being so frank about the pregnancy of this young girl. I was amazed.

It wasn't until the end, when the cast credits came up, that I realized this wasn't a documentary at all; Taylor had written the script, and these were all actors. I thought, "Wow, this guy has talent."

We found out later that the Academy also thought he had talent; *Teenage Father* won an Oscar for best short film, live action.

We met with Taylor and were very impressed. We brought him in to meet with David Field, who agreed to hire him to do the rewrites on *The Idolmaker,* with the understanding that if the new draft worked, Taylor could direct his first feature. David felt comfortable with a first-timer because he knew I had worked with several great first-time directors, including Warren Beatty, Robert Benton, Jim Bridges, Gene Saks, and Paul Mazursky. After Taylor's rewrites were in, David green lit the first movie Gene and I ever made as producing partners.

There were two important exterior scenes in the script that I knew needed careful handling: one at the Fulton Fish Market, in Manhattan, and one on Arthur Avenue, in the Bronx.

Before I got on *Marathon Man,* I'd learned that the producers had tried to use the Fulton Fish Market but had run into trouble. They had gotten all the city permits, and after spending four hours lighting, they were finally ready to shoot when a fleet of trucks drove right in front of the camera and stopped dead right there.

When the AD ran up and told them the film crew had a permit to shoot, he was laughed at and told that while he may have a city permit, he didn't get one from them. "Them" meant the boys, you know, who owned the action at the Fulton Fish Market.

That caused all sorts of problems on *Marathon Man,* and I was determined it would not get in my way on *The Idolmaker.* I knew the one person I should call was Bernie Styles.

I had known Bernie since 1962, when he worked for my father as the extras casting director on *The Manchurian Candidate.*

When my father was about to make that film, Frank Sinatra told him to hire Bernie as his extras casting person. Bernie had never done it before, but he learned the ropes fast and became great at it.

He was only five feet and change, but he was most assuredly a fireball of energy, a force to be reckoned with. You didn't want to be on the wrong side of Bernie. He became the top extras casting person in New York, and he always knew the right people to talk to so there'd be no trouble on a shoot.

Bernie worked on many movies for my dad and would have done anything for him. In the '70s, he also began working for me. He was as loyal to the Koch family as any man could be, and I trusted him completely.

When we began to prep *The Idolmaker,* I called Bernie and asked him if he knew anybody who could get us the right permission to shoot at the Fulton Fish Market and on Arthur Avenue.

"Yeah, sure, you gotta go meet some guys I know, sweetheart."

Bernie arranged for the two of us to meet with Carly and Junior (I kid you not) at a restaurant at the Fulton Fish Market.

He said, "Meet me at three tomorrow afternoon." Bernie and I arrived first and waited in a red banquette. It was a scene right out of film noir—an empty restaurant, one bartender whose eyes never looked up as he kept wiping the bar clean in one perpetually shiny spot.

The silence that had been begging for trouble broke when Carly and Junior walked in and sat down directly across from us. Junior, a bit overweight with a two-day growth of beard, must have been in his fifties, a big man and definitely the rougher of the two. He boasted a few scars on his head. Carly, who seemed about forty years old, was dapper; he wore a diamond pinky ring and smoked a very thin, but very long, cigar. He wore an iridescent green suit.

I told them I needed to film one night at the fish market and one day on Arthur Avenue.

Carly looked at me with ice-cold eyes and said, "That could be arranged. How much do you want to pay me?" which is when I started stammering and speaking way too fast.

"Well, it's a low-budget movie, Carly, so I really don't know what to offer you. We don't have a lot of money for locations. But I don't want to insult you."

"I don't want you to insult me either," Carly said, before adding, "You're going to get everything you want at both places. So how much do you want to pay me?"

This was merely a business deal to them, and they knew they held all the cards.

No matter how far over my head I was in—and man, was I in over my head—I decided I better come up with an offer quick.

"How about five thousand dollars a day, or ten thousand for the two days?"

"No, that doesn't work. It'll cost you twenty-five thousand dollars cash. Get me twelve thousand and five hundred dollars in small bills tomorrow. Bring it in a briefcase, and I'll tell you where to deliver it. You'll give me the other twelve thousand and five hundred dollars on the first night of shooting."

I looked at Bernie, he nodded, then I turned to Carly and gave him the only response possible. "Yes, sir."

Now I had to go see the head of business affairs at United Artists, Dean Stolber, and tell him that I needed $12,500 in small bills to secure locations for *The Idolmaker*.

When I did just that, Dean said exactly what I expected: "Are you out of your friggin' mind? We don't do that."

I told him the whole story, and I could see he was starting to cave when he asked me questions like, "How do you know you'll have it?"

This time I told him with confidence, "Because if Bernie Styles says it's gonna happen, it will. There's no one more well connected on the street than Bernie." And so it did. The Fulton Fish Market shoot went off without a hitch.

A few days later we went to Arthur Avenue, and once again had total control of the street, including all the Italian restaurants, absolutely everything, as promised.

Sonny was a guy who owned a bakery on Arthur Avenue and it had to be shut down that last day in order for us to film. He approached me at the end of the day's shooting and said, "Hey, Mr. Koch, how about a little something extra for me? I didn't have any clients today because you shut down the street."

I told him, "Honestly, Sonny, I made the deal with Carly. He said he would take care of everybody. I wish I could, but I'm not going against what Carly said. Maybe you should talk to him."

"Oh, I'll talk to Carly all right," he said with an edge.

A few days later I spoke with Bernie and asked him, "Hey, whatever happened with that guy Sonny, who wanted money for shutting down his bakery?"

Bernie said, "Oh, yeah, that was a real shame. His bakery burned down."

★ ★ ★

In the early '60s, Phil Spector transformed the pop record industry by turning so-called bubblegum music into his more sophisticated Wall of Sound, which he described as a Wagnerian approach to rock 'n' roll. Every song he produced had an orchestra behind it, including The Ronettes's "Be My Baby," The Righteous Brothers's "You've Lost That Lovin' Feeling," and George Harrison's "My Sweet Lord." We were excited that we had a genius like him set to write the songs for *The Idolmaker*.

Taylor, Gene, and I would frequently go to Phil's house during prep so he could play us the various songs he was writing for the movie. He lived just above the Sunset Strip, in a house surrounded by a huge fence topped with an imposing band of I-dare-you-to-come-in barbed wire. Once we pressed the buzzer, we'd be met by his security guard, who was always dressed in a Hawaiian shirt and sometimes greeted us with a parrot on his shoulder.

The guard would escort us into Phil's two-story living room, which was utterly dark since it was cloaked with heavy drapes from floor to ceiling. Eventually, Phil would amble in, dressed entirely in black, with a gun visibly sticking out above the waist of his pants. That unnerved us, to say the least.

Phil led us into a room off the main living area that had a pool table and, beyond that, into the hallway, where a grand piano stood. Each time we went, he'd play us a song, and Gene, Taylor, and I would get more and more excited. On one of those visits, Phil had Darlene Love, whose big hit was "Today I Met the Boy I'm Gonna Marry," sing the songs. The day we heard her sing, we knew we were gonna have great music for our movie.

In the meantime, we had been talking with Phil's music attorney, since we needed the rights to the masters in order to use the songs in the film. One time, I said to Phil, "The attorney's gotta close this up. We're only four weeks away from shooting. We still have to prerecord all this music with our stars, but we can't do that unless we own the masters." He looked at me and said somewhat dismissively, "Oh, don't worry." A little warning bell went off in me when he said that, so when we got back to our office, the first thing I did was call his music attorney. He gave me the news I did not want to hear: "Howard, Phil's never gonna sign away his music."

That was a disappointment that blew us all the way back to square one. We'd spent months with Phil, and we were set to start shooting. We thought we were screwed until someone had the brilliant idea that we contact Jeff Barry. Jeff was another great songwriter of the late '50s and early '60s, who (along with Ellie Greenwich and Phil) had written hits like "Do Wah Diddy Diddy," "Da Doo Ron Ron," "Then He Kissed Me," "Be My Baby," "Chapel of Love," and "River Deep–Mountain High."

We got ahold of Jeff, and after he read and decided he loved the script, he came over to our tiny production office. We had an upright piano there, and within days, not weeks, Jeff had written absolutely the right kind of songs, music, and lyrics for *The Idolmaker*. They were so perfect that my kids are still singing those songs almost forty years later.

Gene always used to say, "What we need is a jump shot at the buzzer." Jeff Barry hit that jump shot!

28

In 1981 Gene and I outbid both Robert Redford's and Dustin Hoffman's companies for the rights to the novel *Gorky Park,* and because we were able to do that, we mistook ourselves for hot young producers. We almost lost our shirts—and our houses—but let me back up.

Gorky Park is the story of an investigator on the Moscow police force in search of the solution to a triple homicide that occurred in Moscow's Gorky Park. No one really wants him to solve the crime because it's part of an intricate conspiracy involving the highest levels of the city's government.

Detective movies with complicated plots were a dime a dozen, but no one had ever seen one about a Russian cop. We bought the rights, banking on the fact that an American audience would love it. The deal directly tied the compensation of the book's author, Martin Cruz Smith, to the book's performance on the best-seller list. It was such a great story we felt confident we'd be able to "lay it off"—get a financier to pick it up—quick.

To our great pleasure, it did indeed make the best-seller list. To our great dismay, it stayed there for a long time, steadily increasing the amount of money we owed Cruz Smith. To our surprise, disappointment, and eventual gut-wrenching fear, no financier wanted to pick up the rights to the book.

We decided to say to Dustin, "Since you love the book, c'mon, be in it with us." And Dustin decided to say right back, "Nope." Ditto Redford. Meanwhile, the money Gene and I owed was approaching a million dollars.

Neither of us had anywhere near that kind of money, so as you can imagine we were scared out of our wits. My marriage to Marcia began to suffer even more strain than it was already burdened with.

Still, Gene and I had a lot of proverbial irons in the fire in addition to *Gorky Park*, and we were optimistic all our movies would get made. We had purchased the rights to *The Pope of Greenwich Village*, a cult-classic book everybody loved. We were also developing a movie about Chippendales male dancers called *Ladies Night*, which had been written by Joan Tewkesbury, the screenwriter of *Nashville*. To the outside world we looked like hot producers, but inside we were quaking in our loafers.

Enter my father.

I had told my dad the predicament we were in. He called me one day to say he'd met a guy named Uri Harkham. Not only did Uri love *Gorky Park*, but my dad told me he was interested in getting into the film business.

Gene, great salesman that he is, and I met with Uri and ultimately made a deal for him and his brother to become executive producers, an arrangement that took us out of our vulnerable position until we were lucky enough to lay it off. While the pressure was off us personally, it was replaced with a different kind of pressure. Gene had sold Uri and his brother on our certainty that we could get it set up, but the truth was that the more time went by, the less certain we really were that we could do it.

We had two meetings set up in one day; one in the morning with Dino De Laurentiis, and the other in the afternoon with Mike Medavoy, at Orion Pictures. We went to Dino's house first to meet with him and Fred Sidewater, Dino's consigliere. I knew Dino because in 1977 he'd wanted me to be Roman Polanski's eyes and ears for a location scout in Bora Bora for the film *Hurricane,* which

Roman was set to direct. Roman was in the Chino jail at the time and prep needed to start. Marcia and I were at LAX getting ready to board our flight to Bora Bora when a big meaty hand grabbed my shoulder. It was Fred Sidewater telling me, "We're not using Roman. We've decided to hire Jan Troell to direct." Damn, we wanted to take that trip.

★ ★ ★

Dino said, "So you own this *Gorky Park*?"

When we assured him we did, he said, "I understand nobody wants to make it."

"That's not entirely true," Gene said. "We still have a lot of interest."

This is called posturing. Or what others might call bullshit. But Dino made an offer.

"I'll tell you what: I'll take it off your hands. You have nothing more to do with it. If the movie gets made, I'll give you each a hundred grand. If it doesn't get made, then it's my problem."

We thanked him for the offer and told him we'd think about it. Gene and I walked outside to the car, and then Gene said to me, "Hey, I wouldn't let Stallone sell his script, and I'm not gonna let us give up on this one either."

We headed to Medavoy's office, hoping for better luck.

Mike said, "I like the book, but you gotta have a filmmaker on it. Who's that gonna be, because I'm not going to pick it up it unless you have a great filmmaker."

I told Mike, "Billy Friedkin's interested."

Mike was surprised and said, "He is? If you can get Billy in here this afternoon and he can tell me himself he wants to make the movie, I'll make the deal."

I called Billy, who I knew loved the book, and he agreed to come in. As soon as he told Medavoy he thought he could make a good film, we had a deal. Suddenly Gene and I could breathe again, and Uri and his brother were in the movie business.

I will always be indebted to the Harkhams, who I believe just might have saved me from having a heart attack from all the stress I was under. But even more gratitude belongs to my father. He may never have known how to relate on a personal level, and he may have cast a shadow that often rendered me invisible, but he also always came through in a clutch professionally.

Even though we didn't make any movies in 1981, Gene and I were out there putting a lot of projects together. We worked and worked, but no money was coming in. With my three kids, child support, alimony for Rita, and Marcia and I spending money we didn't have, my marriage became more and more wobbly. True to form, I ignored it by shoving it down into that gaping hole where I'd been hiding all my troubles for as long as I could remember, and I poured myself even more thoroughly into my work.

In early 1982 we caught a break. A project we had been developing called *The Keep*, with the young director Michael Mann, went into turnaround from CBS Films on a Friday. We sent the screenplay out to the town that night, and by early Saturday morning, Jeffrey Katzenberg and Michael Eisner called us and asked us to come to Paramount right away. They made a deal with us that day, and suddenly we had a "go picture" to produce.

By that summer Marcia, Robby, and I moved to London to prep *The Keep*, while Gene stayed home and continued to develop some of our other projects. Michael is a great filmmaker but was not particularly interested in my input. Although we get along great today, we butted heads constantly back then. Meanwhile, I was still prepping *Gorky Park* while I was in London.

I called Katzenberg to let him know not only how bad the relationship between Michael and me was, but more importantly to say that I didn't believe his rewriting of the script was improving it. And I added, I believed that his way of working was going to skyrocket our budget. Jeffrey said, "We believe in Michael's vision. Why don't you go ahead and make *Gorky Park* and leave *The Keep?*" I was happy with that decision.

The film cost a lot more than we all had hoped and was critically slammed, and it tanked at the box office.

29

Even though Billy Friedkin had said yes to direct *Gorky Park* in Medavoy's office (and got Mike to work with us to develop the film), by the time we got ready to make it, Billy had stepped away. Michael Apted, who had done *Coal Miner's Daughter,* was now set to direct. Dennis Potter had written a terrific screenplay, and William Hurt and Lee Marvin were set to star. We began looking for the right actress to play Irina, the female lead.

I called Roman Polanski in France and told him, "I'm looking for an Eastern European actress who speaks English. Do you know of anyone?"

The role was for a Russian female who will do anything to get out of the Soviet Union. I specifically wanted an Eastern European actress to play the role because only someone who'd lived under Soviet rule would understand the circumstances of our character.

Roman said, "Oh, Howie, I don't know. If I think of someone, I will call you back."

The next day he called. "I have an idea," he said. "There's this actress Joanna Pacula. She's Polish, and she speaks nine languages. She just moved to America."

"Is one of those languages English?" I asked hopefully.

"She didn't before, but she probably does now because she picks them up quickly."

"Is she beautiful and can she act?"

"Yes, she's beautiful, and she's a very good actress."

Roman gave me her number. When she answered her phone, speaking English and proving Roman right once again, I said, "Hi, my name is Howard Koch, and I'm a film producer. I'm producing a movie called *Gorky Park*."

She surprised me by saying, "Oh, I just read the book."

"Great," I said. "That's great. My director and my star are in New York, and I'd like to arrange for you to meet them."

After he met her, Apted called me and said, "Oh, my God, she's gorgeous and she's perfect for the role—if she can act. You gotta meet her."

I flew to New York and set up a meeting for twelve thirty with Joanna at the Russian Tea Room. I met her, and there was an immediate attraction between us.

Joanna was as smart as she was captivatingly beautiful. She was also rough and unpolished, and she spoke a self-taught English. I was intoxicated by her. It wasn't just her beauty and naïveté that I was drawn to. I didn't know it then, but I was drunk on the idea of being her hero.

Even though I was smitten, I told Apted, Medavoy, and Arthur Krim (the head man at Orion) that we needed to test her to see if she could act. It wasn't surprising that she turned out to be the best, because in some ways she was living her own version of the story we'd be telling in the movie.

Joanna had left Poland to do a television commercial in Paris. At that exact time, the Polish government had closed their border, so she knew if she went home she'd never get out again. Her personal political dilemma helped her to understand the character of Irina Asanova. It was exciting when everyone was in agreement that we'd found our actress.

Finally, we had our cast, but I had the secret complication of knowing that given our mutual attraction, it would be difficult to stay away from Joanna.

I headed to Helsinki to prep. We tried to keep our affair under wraps, but when Medavoy arrived a month into shooting, he whispered to me, "Hey, I hear she's having an affair with somebody. Who is it?"

I looked at him and confessed, "Me, Mike. It's me," to which he replied a beautifully uncomplicated and nonjudgmental, "Oh."

While a movie set always has been a place where I have felt at home and creatively alive, it is also a place full of sexual energy and tension. We've all read about actors who fall in love on movie sets, but it doesn't just happen to actors. It can—and does—happen to anyone who doesn't see it for what it really is: a pretend environment, full of facades and tempting make-believe. It's so exciting and stimulating that homelife can seem dull in comparison. I did not always remember that.

While in Helsinki, I got a call from my mom. She and I were making small talk. I got caught up on what they were doing, and after telling her a little about how my movie was going and complaining about the freezing weather in Finland, totally out of character, she said, "Let me put Dad on the phone."

That threw me because it was such a rare occurrence, it might have been the day hell froze over.

My dad took the phone and said, "Hey, Howie, how's it going over there? What's going on with the movie?"

I was trying to recover my equilibrium and made every effort to pretend like speaking directly to him instead of through my mother was normal, so I said, "It's going well, Dad. It's just cold, that's all."

Then he got to his point. "I hear things, Howe, and I just want to say—don't let an actress ruin your life."

I'm not sure how many seconds it took me to recover from hearing the first fatherly advice I was ever offered, apart from "Always give a firm handshake." I felt the red heat of shame explode in my body.

I don't know how he knew except to say, again, that Hollywood is a very small town. It doesn't matter if you're working within its city limits or all the way across the world in Finland; eventually, everybody knows your secrets.

My discomfort and shame forced the kind of paralysis that allowed me to brush it off by saying, "Oh, don't worry, Dad. I'm fine."

But I was anything but fine. I was absolutely torn in two. When we finished the film and I got back to California, I couldn't eat or sleep. Joanna was in New York and I was back home, trying to figure out what to do with my life. I could not ignore the reality and the commitment I had made to my marriage and to my family. This was my life. I knew exactly the trajectory I was on, and it was the one I signed up for.

On the other hand, I was Odysseus hearing the Sirens' song, but I was not lashed to the mast and was therefore utterly unable to stay away from Joanna.

As excruciatingly painful as it was to leave my young son, I decided I had to if I was going to be true to myself. Marcia and I had a gut-wrenching encounter that ended when I picked up a few things and went to stay at the second home of a friend of mine until I found a place of my own to live. Joanna came out from New York, and we moved into a little house on Peck Drive, a block and a half from Marcia and close enough to Rita so that I could be near my older kids.

In spite of the indescribable personal anguish, 1983 was the year I began to live—not the life of my parents that I had prescribed for myself, but my own life, determined by my own values, not theirs or anyone else's. I was fulfilled creatively, since my work as the producer involved the script, the actors, and the entire film. I felt empowered, but it was difficult to reconcile that with the knowledge of what I had destroyed to find myself.

I was no longer the good son following in the footsteps of his untainted father. From the time I was old enough to figure it out, I had tried to get it right, had tried to measure up to my father's image. By this time, I knew I couldn't do that.

30

Suddenly Koch/Kirkwood was on a roll. We had Francis Ford Coppola to direct *The Pope of Greenwich Village* with Jimmy Caan and Al Pacino. We were making deals with Lesley Ann Warren and John Avildsen (who had directed *Rocky*) for our *Ladies Night* project, which Gene would supervise in Florida while I was in Helsinki with *Gorky Park*.

But unexpected changes began to happen to some of our movie projects. Jimmy Caan, Francis Coppola, and Al Pacino exited *The Pope*. Now we had Eric Roberts, Mickey Rourke, and a young director named Ron Maxwell. Just when I came home from Finland, and Joanna and I moved in together, I had to turn right around and go back to New York because *The Pope* was a go. After spending a couple of weeks there, I felt strongly that Ron Maxwell was not the right director for this movie.

Peter Bart, who later became editor of *Daily Variety*, was the creative exec at MGM at the time the movie was being made. The hierarchy at MGM included Peter, Freddie Fields as head of production, and Frank Yablans as head of the studio. I went to see Peter, who told me that even though he agreed with me about Maxwell, Frank Yablans loved him, so it wasn't likely we could get him off the movie.

On day one of rehearsal, Ron Maxwell came to Gene and me at lunch and told us that he didn't believe Eric Roberts was a good enough actor to play the role of Paulie. He wanted to recast the part. Gene and I told Ron, "We believe in Eric, and we're not letting him go." Ron followed that up with an ultimatum: "It's either him or me." That gave us an opening, so I immediately called Peter Bart and told him the situation. Peter thought that with this info, added to the fact that the movie Maxwell had just directed for Yablans was unreleasable, he could get Yablans to agree to let us fire him. The problem was we were two weeks away from shooting and needed a director immediately.

I had worked as an AD on several movies with Stuart Rosenberg, who had directed *Cool Hand Luke*. He had just recently taken over from Bob Rafelson on the film *Brubaker,* and the movie was a great success. Stuart had been brought up in New York and knew the city well. He had directed lots of television before becoming a film director, including the New York–centric *Naked City.* He was the perfect choice. I immediately called his agent, Lenny Hirshan, and sent him the script.

Freddie Fields screamed at me for having the audacity to send Stuart's agent the script because Freddie himself had a director in mind and intended to bring him on. I said, "But, Freddie, I'm the producer, and I also have a responsibility to find the person I think is the right director."

Freddie was bringing his guy into New York the next day, and we were to meet with him at the MGM apartment. When we got there, Freddie introduced us to Michael Cimino, who had won an Oscar for directing *The Deer Hunter* and was infamous for directing *Heaven's Gate,* the film that threw United Artists into bankruptcy.

Although Michael had just received the script as he got on the plane, by the time we met him at the apartment, his copy looked like it had been worked on for six months. Every page was dog-eared, stained, and covered in notes. We brought him up to date on our progress. He asked if we had taken our two stars and our sound mixer equipped with radio mics to all 185 of our New York locations to

make sure we'd get good sound, since as he informed us, "I don't loop."
Uh-oh, I thought. We're in trouble here.

By ten the next morning, Michael came into our production office
and told us that because it was clear to him we weren't properly prepared, he would not be doing our film. Bullet dodged.

When Freddie Fields found out Cimino wouldn't do it, he said, "I
have a great idea who should direct this film: Stuart Rosenberg." He
was not joking. He was dead serious that it was his idea. In the end,
what mattered was that Stuart came in and did a fantastic job directing *The Pope of Greenwich Village*.

While I was prepping *The Pope* in New York, I got a call from Ray
Stark. He loved *The Idolmaker* and was looking for somebody to run
his company. Would I fly out to LA and meet with him? Yes, I would.

I met with him in a little Chinese restaurant in Toluca Lake. He
said, "I haven't made a movie in two years. I want my company back
in action again."

Given the fact that another of my marriages had broken up, that I
was about to have another four-month stay in New York on *The Pope,*
and that producing movies would always keep me away from my
family, Ray's offer seemed like a godsend. It would give me an office
in LA, and I'd have a stable job with a stable salary. To be president of
Rastar would also be a prestigious leap in my career. But most importantly, I'd be able to stay in town and be near my family.

I flew back to New York to talk to Gene. I sat down with him and
told him about Ray's offer. I finished by saying, "Gene-o, with three
kids and two ex-wives, I won't be able to run around from movie to
movie anymore. I hope you can understand that."

True to form, he did. With all the grace that Gene possesses—and
that's a lot—he said, "Sure, of course, I understand. You gotta go, baby."

Gene always was, and still is, a good guy and he is my friend to
this day.

Becoming the head of Rastar was a move that suddenly rendered
me visible when most of my life I had felt quite the opposite. It's just

that the juicier news that I had left my wife for a young actress over-shadowed the good publicity about my becoming head of Rastar.

★ ★ ★

I was struggling to know how to be a father to my children. Understanding my parental shortcomings, I always tried to come up with things that they'd enjoy, and then I'd do those things with them. With Billy it was always sports, so that was easy. I had a much harder time figuring out what Emily might enjoy.

But I do remember once really nailing it. While I was working at Rastar, our deal was at Columbia Pictures. I was invited to the premiere of *Ghostbusters*, which was going to be held on a Sunday morning. I knew I wanted to bring Emily, who was eleven at the time, because she was in love with Rob Lowe and I knew he was going to be at the premiere. Emily was thrilled when I invited her. Without telling her anything about Rob Lowe, I'd arranged it so that she'd be sitting next to him in the theater. We walked the red carpet and then went inside. We sat in our seats and were talking to one another when shortly before the movie started, Rob Lowe walked up to say hello. I introduced Emily and still remember the look of surprise and puppy love on her young face. But when he sat down next to her, I thought those same eyes might pop right out of their sockets, she was so excited. I had clued Rob in ahead of time, and he couldn't have been kinder. As if she wasn't thoroughly enjoying herself already, there was a party afterward where I'd arranged for us to sit at the same table as Rob.

I will never forget what she did when we came back to my house afterward. Emily hurled herself on the king-size bed and promptly did a full feet-over-head body flip. As a dad, and a fairly inept one at that, other than the unconditional love I had for her, I couldn't do a lot. But I knew I could do this, and I think it made me as happy as it made her.

31

The first thing I had to do in my new role as president of Rastar was to put together a staff. I asked my friend David Field if he knew anybody who was a great developer who could work as my vice president. David, one of the smartest men I know, introduced me to someone equal to him in brain power: Paul Gurian. Not only did I like Paul, but I was also a fan of a movie he produced called *Cutter's Way*. Paul and I got along great. Ray thought he was a little odd because he had a long ponytail and a giant walruslike mustache, but despite those reservations, Ray liked him too.

We started finding and developing material.

When I got the job at Rastar, I was finally able to buy a home of my own again. I bought a four-bedroom house in Benedict Canyon so that Billy, who was fourteen; Emily, who was eleven; and Robby, who was five, could each have their own room. Robby had a red, race-car bed. Just as I had when I was growing up, they each had their own TV. It was their house too and they made the most of it.

Joanna's driving force was work. She was getting calls to audition for leads in European productions, but her Polish passport had expired and the Polish consulate would not renew it. Her being unable to go frustrated her. As time went by, it became a real problem for her—and by extension—for me.

We knew that the only way for her to travel out of the country was if she was married to an American citizen. Working was more important to her than marriage, but it seemed she couldn't have one without the other. And, we were in love. So...in spite of how absolutely certain I was that I would never do it again, we eloped to Vegas.

Joanna auditioned for a big movie but didn't get the part. The producer persuaded her to believe that I wouldn't be happy about her being away in Mexico for sixteen weeks. That, of course, left Joanna certain I was the reason she wasn't getting work, while it left me certain that the producer found a way to refuse her the job without taking responsibility for his decision by laying it off on me. Thanks, pal.

The fact is—and I told Joanna this—I would never have stood in the way of her doing what she loved. After all, I married her so she could do just that.

★ ★ ★

Ray had made a play-or-pay deal with the hot actor of the day, Tom Hanks, to star in a movie that was to be written by Neil Simon. It would be based on Simon's hit Broadway musical comedy *They're Playing Our Song*.

When Neil's screenplay came in, both Ray and I read it. When Ray asked me what I thought, I told him frankly, "I think it's terrible. Nobody is gonna make this movie."

Ray's response was even franker. "Bullshit," he said. "We're gonna get it to Tom Hanks, and he has to do it. We are gonna make it. It's Neil Simon, for God's sake! Neil's my friend. He'll fix whatever is wrong."

"Okay, Ray" was all that was left to say.

Meanwhile, I got a call from my friend Amy Grossman, an agent at CAA. Amy knew we had Tom Hanks, so she said, "Listen, there's a script that just came out. I think Michael and Kirk Douglas are thinking about it but I doubt they'll do it. Maybe it's something you'd want to put together for Tom Hanks."

I told her Tom was doing *They're Playing Our Song* but then added, "Let me read it over the weekend."

On the following Monday morning, we sent Neil Simon's script to Tom and his agents. By the end of the week, Tom's people said, "Tom is not doing this film."

Ray's response was typical Ray when he was pushed up against a wall. He huffed and puffed. "If Tom doesn't do this movie, he'll never work in this town again. I've got an iron-clad pay-or-play deal with him for this film. He has to do it!"

I went to Ray and told him, "I read a script last weekend called *Nothing in Common*. It would be great for Tom. It's a father-and-son story. If you could have your friend Jackie Gleason play the father, we might get out of our problem with Tom."

After Ray read the script, he told me to, "Go to the Morris office. You talk to Alan Iezman, Tom's agent, and you tell him straight, 'There's only one way we'll let Tom out of *They're Playing Our Song*, and that's if he commits—pay-or-play—to this one.'"

I walked into the meeting with Jerry Lipsky, a tough-as-nails attorney whose one client was Ray Stark. Jerry really laid into Alan Iezman and Ed Liebowitz, William Morris's head of business affairs. Jerry led with a bunch of hard-ass lawyer stuff. Then I moved in by saying, "But there's one script that *maybe* we'd consider doing with Tom."

Iezman interrupted by saying, "Before you tell us about that one, Tom read a script over the weekend, and he'd commit to that one if you want to make it."

"What is it?" I asked.

"It's called *Nothing in Common*."

Jerry and I looked at each other—all the tension gone now—and laughed. We had our movie, and now we had our star too.

We were very proud of the movie we made. Garry Marshall directed it, and Alexandra Rose produced it. It was written by my old Pony League pal Rick Podell and his partner, Michael Preminger.

There's a scene at the end where Gleason is going into an operating room. I shared the transformative moment I had with my father at the Mayo Clinic when he grabbed my arm before being wheeled into the operating room. Touched, they wrote that scene into the script. Jackie put his hand on Tom's forearm, and there was a genuine and powerful moment between them—just as occurred between my father and me.

***

Soon after that, we made a deal with TriStar to make *Peggy Sue Got Married,* about a thirty-six-year-old woman traveling back in time to high school, knowing what she knows now and trying to figure out why she married her high school sweetheart. Because Paul Gurian had brought the project to Rastar, he was no longer going to be my vice president; he was going to be the producer of *Peggy Sue.*

The film takes place in small-town America. We got Jonathan Demme to direct and Debra Winger to star. During the development process, it became evident that Demme and Winger had creative differences. It got so serious that at some point they had gotten into a nonnegotiable argument that boiled down to "it's either her or me."

Paul and I went to Ray and told him we thought he should stick with the director. Jonathan Demme really understood the material. He went on to make *The Silence of the Lambs* and *Philadelphia.* We knew how much talent he had, but we hadn't taken into consideration that Gary Hendler, who was now head of TriStar, represented Debra Winger when he was a lawyer.

Hendler insisted on keeping Winger, not Demme, which meant I had to find another director. The next week, Gary Hendler called me to come to his office for a meeting. I walked in to see Debra Winger and Penny Marshall sitting on his couch kibitzing with one another. I was sand-bagged. I walked into a room where the decision had already been made that Rastar was going to produce a movie that Gary Hendler had decided was going to be directed by Penny Marshall.

I knew Penny had never directed anything other than a couple of episodes of *Laverne & Shirley* so I wasn't too excited about the prospect of her taking over for Jonathan Demme, and neither was Paul Gurian. It's just that we had no choice in the matter.

Within a week or two, it was complete chaos. Penny worked all hours and wanted to schedule meetings at midnight. One night I awoke to someone throwing pebbles at my bedroom window. It was the writers at one in the morning. They had just come from a meeting with Penny. They were dismayed, nearly in tears in fact, because she, coming from the Bronx, didn't get why this screenplay needed to be set in middle America. Penny wanted to set it in the Bronx. The writers played an audio tape for me from a meeting they had just had. Penny was asking to revise the script in ways that made it clear this wasn't going to be the movie we wanted to make.

It made so little sense that I went in to see Ray the next day and after filling him in said, "C'mon, Ray, this is not the movie we signed up to do. We've got to fire Penny."

Ray agreed but looked at me and said, "Okay, I'll talk to Hendler, but you better get a fucking great director because Penny is Gary Hendler's choice, and he's not gonna like this."

We were able to get Penny off the film, and luckily soon after, the phone rang. It was Barry Hirsch, of the law firm Armstrong/Hirsch. Barry said, "Hey, have you got any projects for Francis Coppola? He's in some financial trouble, and he could really use a film right now."

Talk about the stars aligning.

I said, "Have I got a film for him? You bet I do."

We sent Francis *Peggy Sue Got Married* and not only did he love the script, but we could shoot it up in Santa Rosa right next to where he lived in Napa. It was perfect...until it wasn't.

We were in a budget meeting at TriStar—head of production Jeff Sagansky, their young production executive Gary Lucchesi, Francis, Paul Gurian, and me—about seven weeks from shooting, when I was pulled out of the meeting for a telephone call.

"Rick Nicita's on the phone for you." Rick was Debra Winger's agent.

When I answered, the first words out of Rick's mouth were, "Debra Winger can't work."

"What do you mean she can't work?" I asked incredulously.

Rick explained, "She's got a herniated disc in her back. She's in traction, and can't work for six months."

I walked back in the room, explained what was going on, and suddenly our conversation turned from budgets to casting again. "Who are we gonna get to make this movie now?"

A year earlier *Romancing the Stone* had come out, and we all agreed it would be great if we could get Kathleen Turner, who everyone loved, to play Peggy Sue.

We made a call and found out Kathleen was in Morocco shooting the second film in the *Romancing the Stone* franchise, *The Jewel of the Nile*. We sent her our script, and she committed to it.

Ray knew that Francis, as a creative force, was totally indifferent when it came to paying attention to budgets, so he said to me, "You know more about production than just about anybody. Put a clause in his contract that stipulates he has to make decisions in preproduction in order to keep the film on budget. If he goes over budget, he doesn't get paid."

That inspired me—forced me, actually—to put together a manual of what had to be done by the director in order to be prepared to shoot. It was similar to the way I prepped Mike Nichols for *Bogart Slept Here*. It stipulated that no piece of lumber, no nail could be hammered on any set until the plans had been drawn, estimated, and come in within budget. The director, production designer, producer, and cameraman had to sign those blueprints. The same was true for costumes, locations, and every department on down the line. Every part of making the movie had to be signed off by Francis before we began. At the bottom of his contract was one line that said, "The director has the right to change his mind." He signed.

One of the idiosyncrasies of making movies is that the director's decisions are the ones that the entire crew accepts verbatim.

With that kind of power, it's not uncommon for a director, once he sees what he actually asked for, to then say, "Oh no, I never said that" or "I don't want that. I want something else." That backpedaling/mind-changing causes the budget to skyrocket. The contract that Francis had to sign meant he was going to have to think about every eventuality ahead of time.

That kind of preparation had the effect of rendering unnecessary that line at the end of the contract that said, "The director has the right to change his mind."

While I was there, I was able to watch Francis work. At one point, he called me over and said with confusion in his voice, "None of the crew is asking me any questions."

I was happy to reassure him. "That's the idea—because you've prepped everything. The only thing you have to worry about now is the actors and where to put your camera."

"Oh, I kind of like that," he said.

I've used that formula on every movie since *Peggy Sue,* and with one or two exceptions, the movies I've done since 1985 have come in on or under budget. We've prepared the director, and it's a great communication tool for everybody who's working on the film because, without question, they all know what the director's vision is. *Peggy Sue* was nominated for three Oscars, one of which was for Kathleen's portrayal of Peggy Sue.

32

I felt helpless where my kids were concerned. I would pick them up—first Billy and Emily from Rita's, then Robby from Marcia's, and they'd spend the night with me on Friday and Saturday. When I dropped them off at their respective homes, often I would sit in my car asking myself, "What have I done to my children?"

I wasn't just insecure about my role as a single dad; I started to see that my relationships with women often determined how I felt about myself. When I was being appreciated and noticed, I felt good, and when I wasn't, I felt bad.

Joanna began to lose confidence that I wanted to be with her. After all, I had left my wife for her, and she was worried I would do the same to her. She was wrong. I wasn't interested in other women.

During the filming of *Peggy Sue*, Francis threw a party for the whole crew on his Napa property. Joanna and I flew up there, and as we walked in, Kathleen Turner came up to me, gave me a peck on the cheek, and thanked me for casting her. She was having a ball, she said. When she walked away, Joanna looked at me and said, "Let's get out of here. I don't want to be here anymore. Kathleen wants to sleep with you." I said, "No, Joanna. No she doesn't. That's just a movie star expressing her gratitude for the part. That's all it is." I felt defeated. We didn't stay long at that party. By the time we flew back to LA, the writing was on the wall.

Things continued to unravel with Joanna and me, despite our best efforts to stay together. It didn't help that some people would ask her, "Why isn't Howard putting you in movies or developing them for you?"

The answer to this question—which I've had to explain to other women who expected the same of me—is that I never considered it my responsibility to develop material for them just because I was a producer and they were actors. In fact, the question served to make me wonder whether the women for whom this expectation arose were with me for me or because they hoped, or believed, I would advance their careers.

★ ★ ★

The premiere of *Amazing Grace and Chuck* was set to open the AFI Film Festival at Grauman's Chinese Theatre. Both Gary Lucchesi and I had gone out on a limb to get this movie made for our pal David Field, who had written and produced it. This was a really important night for us and the culmination of all that work.

Amazing Grace and Chuck is about a Little League player named Chuck, who lives in Bozeman, Montana. Chuck refuses to pitch again until nuclear weapons are disarmed. Hearing about the boy's boycott, basketball star "Amazing Grace" Smith follows his example and sparks a trend. It's a compelling story about integrity that, come to think of it, we could benefit from seeing today.

In the midst of the premiere, Joanna and I got in an argument that didn't just ruin the night; it ultimately ruined our relationship.

Along with that painful separation, our family suffered some bad news: for several weeks my sister had been experiencing bad cramps and finally went to the doctor. It turned out she had third-stage ovarian cancer. She immediately had surgery, followed by chemotherapy. Her prognosis was not good but Melinda, staying true to her spunkiness, was determined to beat cancer. Her doctors still can't believe that she did, but she has remained clear for thirty-two years,

After recovering from the split with Joanna, I began dating without any intention of getting serious—pretty much ever again. With very few exceptions, I would see someone for a month at the most, more likely a week, and sometimes just a night.

33

Things were going really well at Rastar. Before I got there, Ray hadn't made a film in two years. In the next two and a half, we made twelve. We'd made *Peggy Sue Got Married* and *Nothing in Common*. A. J. Carothers had come up with *The Secret of My Success* and, with Paul Gurian supervising, had written a great script. Herb Ross was going to direct, and after dealing with both his agent and manager, we'd set Matthew Broderick to play the lead. Matthew had done *WarGames, Ladyhawke,* and, of course, *Ferris Bueller's Day Off,* so we knew he'd be perfect for our lead.

I got a call one afternoon from Matthew's manager informing me that Matthew, for reasons we never learned, had decided not to do the movie even though we were all set to go. Welcome to the movie business. Ray was pissed and let me have it, for as he saw it, I let Matthew get away.

I called my friend David Gersh at the Gersh Agency and said, "You've read *The Secret of My Success.* Who have you got?" David immediately knew. "What about Michael J. Fox?" Brilliant idea. We all loved Michael in *Back to the Future* and felt he'd be great. We got him the script, and as luck (and everything else involved in making things work) would have it, Michael wanted to do it. All of a sudden Ray changed his tune to "Great going, Howard. I love Michael J. Fox."

As we knew he would be, Michael was great in the lead. *The Secret of My Success* became a huge hit.

My deal with Ray included my salary plus the possibility of a bonus. I had received a generous one the year before, and given all the movies we'd made since I signed on, I was expecting a significant one this year as well. To my great disappointment, I got far less than I'd received before. I was insulted and upset by the message it conveyed, even though I didn't know quite what that message was.

There was a particular etiquette with Ray where anything having to do with money or contracts was to go through his lawyer Jerry Lipsky. I contacted Jerry and said, "I don't understand why my bonus is so glaringly small. Ray's made so much money lately, and the company's happening again. We're back to making movies."

Jerry's only explanation was, "Well, that's the way Ray feels."

I wasn't going to leave it at that, so I called the person who was arguably the most influential man in Hollywood—and a friend of Ray's—Mike Ovitz, the head of Creative Artists Agency. I figured he'd know what was going on since Mike spoke to Ray every day.

"Am I crazy, Mike?" I asked, "I think I deserve a lot more. Three years ago, Ray didn't have any movies going, and we've made twelve in that same amount of time. I thought he was happy about that."

Mike was emphatic when he said, "Ray's gotta be crazy. He should be paying you a million dollars a year because you're right; Rastar's back in business. Let me talk to him."

I was relieved and thanked him.

A few days later Mike called me to say, "I've got bad news: it's terminal."

"What do you mean 'it's terminal'?"

"He doesn't want you to be head of the company anymore," Mike explained.

I was shocked, stupefied really, and said, "You're kidding. Why? What happened?"

Mike didn't pull any punches. "Ray doesn't like it that people think the company is yours, not his."

"But that's ridiculous. I work for him, and everybody knows it."

Mike ended the conversation by reiterating, "It is terminal, Howard, but let me find you something else."

A week later, Mike called me. "I can make you a great production deal at De Laurentiis Entertainment. More money, an office in Beverly Hills, development people and assistants for you, anything you want. Dino wants you with him."

That news was flattering and certainly made me feel better than I'd been feeling, so I agreed to meet Dino, but reminded Mike, "I still have a few months left on my contract. Don't you think I better wait until it's officially over?"

Mike said, "Dino wants you right away."

"Well, how am I going to tell Ray?"

Mike reassured me, "I'll tell Ray. I'll call him Saturday morning like I always do and I'll take care of it for you."

I wasn't entirely convinced so I said, "Don't you think I ought to tell him myself?"

Mike said simply, "No, let me do it."

He was Mike Ovitz, so I agreed.

I waited for Mike to call. Finally, my phone rang at nine thirty, but it wasn't Mike Ovitz. It was Jerry Lipsky, Ray's lawyer.

The first words out of his mouth were "How could you do this to Ray after all he's done for you?"

I was completely baffled and could only say, "What? Do what?"

Jerry was clearly pissed when he spit out, "Don't act like you don't know. You have Rick Nicita call him and tell him you're leaving the company!"

"Rick Nicita?" I said totally thrown. "Ovitz was going to call Ray."

"Well, he didn't. Nicita did."

Rick was a well-respected, top agent at CAA, but he was most definitely not the head of the agency. He was a talent agent, and to receive a call from him was a completely different experience than receiving one from Mike Ovitz. I can understand that Ray would have taken it as a gesture of disrespect and one that certainly did not speak well of me.

I've had a lot of years to think about this experience, one that left me feeling betrayed. It's possible that Ray and Mike could have decided that the best thing for Ray would be to announce that "Howard Koch walks out on contract, leaving Ray Stark high and dry." In that scenario, I'm the sonofabitch who shafted him. That plays better than if Ray doesn't renew my contract, since everyone in town was well aware that the company was experiencing a moment of solid success. There are lots of possible explanations.

Eventually I found out this was a pattern of Ray's. Former president of Rastar, Mort Engelberg, who also produced *Smokey and the Bandit* for Ray, got the exact same treatment.

I did move over to De Laurentiis, and I began to develop movies. I was there three or four months when I was called into Dino's office for a meeting with his head of production, Raffaella De Laurentiis, Dino's daughter.

It turned out that Raffaella didn't want to run the company for her dad anymore, so I was offered the job as head of production. My lawyer, and all-around gentleman, Charles Silverberg, made the deal and before I knew what was happening, I was head of De Laurentiis Entertainment.

Things were running smoothly—we were finishing *Bill & Ted's Excellent Adventure,* which we were confident was going to be a big hit, and I was in the middle of negotiating to acquire two other screenplays, *Bull Durham* and *Young Guns.*

But then I got a call: "Dino wants to see you."

When I arrived in Dino's office, he was there with his chief financial officer.

"Hi, guys, what's up?" I asked.

Dino, looking at his CFO, said, "Tell him."

The guy in charge of all the money said, "We're filing for bankruptcy. You can't make any more deals. We're not going to make any more movies."

For the second time in a year, I found myself stupefied. "What? But you just hired me."

I knew that the films they had released before I came aboard had failed, but I didn't know to what extent until I was told, "Our films didn't do well. We're out of money and luck."

I left the office reeling. I called Charles, my attorney, to ask, "What the hell am I going to do now?"

Charles said, "You can't really do anything. You have a contract. They have to pay you, but you can't leave."

Everyone in town knew I couldn't do any business, so I sat there for months, until finally, Charles called to tell me he'd worked it out and I could leave.

My friend Taylor Hackford, who directed the hit film *An Officer and a Gentleman*, had started his own producing/financing company called New Visions. Taylor asked me if I would produce a film he'd developed called *Rooftops*. Robert Wise, who won Oscars for *The Sound of Music* and *West Side Story*, was going to direct, and I was thrilled by the opportunity to work with him.

My son Billy and his friend Josh Levinson were production assistants on the movie. One of the things they had to do was go into New York City's Alphabet City, which was pretty rough at the time, to make sure a vacant lot we were going to use as a location was clean—no trash, no needles, and no other drug paraphernalia. One day I got a call from Billy, who was clearly shaken. "Dad, we just found a dead body in the lot!" They could handle the used needles and syringes, but they drew the line at the decomposing corpse. Like I said, Alphabet City was rough. The film didn't do too well, but working with Robert Wise made it all worthwhile.

After *Rooftops*, Taylor asked me to produce another movie for him, called *The Long Walk Home*, which told the story of the Montgomery bus boycott. The black housekeepers refused to take the bus to the white neighborhoods where they worked and decided to walk instead. But walking meant they arrived late for work, so a lot of the white women—unbeknownst to their husbands—drove into the housekeepers' neighborhoods to pick them up and drove them home before their husbands returned from work.

The movie starred Sissy Spacek and Whoopi Goldberg as employer and employee, respectively. Instead of staying in motels, Sissy, Whoopi, and I wanted to rent houses, so I drove around with Jim, a tall and cordial real estate agent in Montgomery, Alabama, who'd scheduled lots of homes for me to see. Jim and I were greeted at one screen door by an elderly woman, scowling and cranky looking with a face as pinched as a sphincter. She greeted Jim first with her deep Southern drawl.

"Hi, Jim" was all she managed until she took one look at me and, perhaps recognizing my Jewishness, spit, then slammed her door, saying, "This house ain't for rent."

I had sadly grown accustomed to anti-Semitism by then and had developed ways to take these comments in stride, sometimes even with humor. Had I been faster on my feet this time, I might have assuaged her anti-Semitic concerns by clarifying that "Oh, it's not for me, ma'am"—dramatic pause—"It's for Whoopi Goldberg."

One of the most memorable experiences of my life happened just a couple of days before filming began when we all decided to make the same five- or six-mile walk those brave housekeepers did in the 1950s. It was Whoopi's idea.

When we started out, there were just a few of us from the movie company, but as word got out, more and more people joined us, and it was spine-tinglingly thrilling. I was so proud of being a part of that walk, but I was also proud to participate in a movie that highlighted the important civil rights protest.

One of the young extras casting assistants on *The Long Walk Home* stood out because of her kindness to my sons—Billy, who was a production assistant, and Robby, when he came to visit. That young woman was Octavia Spencer, who, over twenty years later, became an Oscar-winning actress. You never know who's going to become the next big star.

* * *

In 1989, the board of governors of the Motion Picture Academy voted for my dad to receive the Jean Hersholt Humanitarian Award. It's an honorary Oscar given for an individual's outstanding contributions to humanitarian causes. He deserved it.

Our whole family went to the Oscar ceremony that year to support him. We were all sitting just a few rows from the stage. It was clear when Dad got up to get his Oscar, after being introduced by his old pal Walter Matthau, that he was nervous. During his speech, he said a little something about each one of us: his wonderful wife, Ruth; his beautiful daughter, Melinda; and his son, Howard. The words he said about me shot straight into me: "One day I hope my son will also be up on this stage getting an Oscar."

I was proud that he acknowledged me in front of the industry audience and the millions of television viewers. I was hit with a mix of sadness and love. My father's very public wish for me was a warm and validating gesture, one I didn't know how to receive.

* * *

This was the year Billy went off to college at Northwestern. I was thrilled when Emily, in need of a change, decided to move into my house permanently, just her and her 276 pairs of white Keds. The kid could put Imelda Marcos to shame.

Mom turned seventy and we gave her a surprise party at the Bistro. I couldn't believe we managed to pull it off without her having a clue, but we did. I guess I was skilled at surprises. Some—like this one for my mom—were even good ones.

34

Every once in a while—usually when you least expect it and are most in need of it—the universe tosses you a big, juicy bone. Mine came courtesy of my good friend Gary Lucchesi.

Gary had been pulled from his position as senior vice president of TriStar to become head of production at Paramount. Once there, he offered me an exclusive producing deal, an opportunity I jumped at.

Necessary Roughness, the first film I made under my deal, was about an older guy who goes back to college. He decides to try out for quarterback on the college team since he was a pretty good player in his day and ends up on the team. The coach announces, "We're gonna have a scrimmage against a really rough team." He isn't kidding because the team they bring up is from the state penitentiary. We hired great ex-football players and one heavyweight champion to play the penitentiary team.

Making this movie was a blast and the perfect thing to share with my football-loving son Robby, who was twelve at the time. He flew from Los Angeles to Denton, Texas, where we were filming. I got to introduce him to some amazing NFL players: guys like Jerry Rice, Jim Kelly, "Big" Ben Davidson, Dick Butkus, Roger Craig, Ed "Too Tall" Jones, Tony Dorsett, Emmitt Smith, and even heavyweight champion Evander Holyfield. We had a ball, and I was happy I got to share that with Robby.

There were lots of things I could never do for my kids, but I could bring them to my sets so they could share those once-in-a-lifetime experiences that only show business has to offer.

While in the midst of shooting, Gary called and asked me to fly to LA to meet Lorne Michaels. Lorne wanted to make a movie called *Wayne's World*, based on the popular *Saturday Night Live* sketch. I had seen a few of the episodes, but what did I know? The first thing I did was call my kids to ask them what they thought of the idea.

All three of them said, "Dad, you gotta do it!"

Based on the sage advice of my children, I met with Lorne, and to my good fortune, I got the job.

By now Billy had graduated from Northwestern University and had worked on enough movie sets with me that I felt confident he could be the key set production assistant. He did a great job, even though his heart was never in the entertainment business. Like his great-grandfather before him, Billy's heart belonged to the racing ponies, and it still does.

A few weeks in, we were shooting the scene with Robert Patrick, who played the cop in *Terminator 2*. It's the moment where he gets off his motorcycle and stops Wayne in the blue Pacer and comes to his window and says something like, "You were speeding."

It was a Friday night shoot, so I brought Robby out to the set with me. I was standing with Penelope Spheeris, the director, and Robby, watching them rehearse the scene.

When Robert Patrick says to Wayne, "You were speeding," Robby, in true kids-say-the-darndest-things fashion, blurted out, "That's not funny."

I wanted to crawl into a hole until Mike Myers looked over at us and saved the day. "Hey, the kid's right," he said. "It's *not* funny."

Upon consultation, my twelve-year-old son informed us that in *Terminator 2*, Robert didn't say anything about speeding but held up a Polaroid and asked, "Have you seen this boy?"

When Robby concluded for all the adults that *that's* what Robert should say to Wayne, Mike agreed. They took a Polaroid of Robby, and when the scene was actually shot, Robert comes up to the blue Pacer with a picture of my son, shows it to Wayne, and says, "Have you seen this boy?"

When the movie opened, Robby's Andy Warhol fifteen minutes of fame got a big laugh and of course he loved the fact that he was in *Wayne's World*—if only by Polaroid. Clever kid. He's now an entertainment lawyer, making deals he probably wished he'd known how to make for himself back then.

During the previews, we got some strong numbers, but when we previewed in Wayne, New Jersey, they flew off the charts. Not only did the audience roar throughout the entire film, but the numbers told us what a giant hit we had on our hands.

Within four weeks of opening, the movie grossed $125 million. No one at Paramount—least of all me—had had a clue just how big a hit *Wayne's World* would be, or how many decades later people would still be quoting *"Wayne's World, Wayne's World, party time!"*

Thanks to Gary, I'm still chewing on that wonderfully tasty bone he threw me all those years ago with *Wayne's World,* and I will always think of that as simply EX-CEL-LENT!

★ ★ ★

Right around this time my son Billy attended the premiere of *Other People's Money* with his buddy Josh, who was working for Danny DeVito at the time. A few weeks after the premiere, Billy did something he rarely did: he sought out my advice. "Hey, Dad, I met this girl at the premiere. I like her. She's a physical fitness expert. She has an extra ticket to London, and she wants me to go with her. Do you think I should do it?" Without hesitating, I said, "Billy, you're twenty-one years old and some girl you like wants to take you to London? Go! Have the time of your life."

They did go, and I guess he did have the time of his life because Billy's been married to Kathy Kaehler for more than twenty years.

It would be years before Kathy fessed up to Billy that she never did have an extra ticket....She bought one just so she could be with him. Well played, Kathy.

35

I was working with Robert Evans again, this time producing *Sliver*, starring Sharon Stone and Billy Baldwin. The end sequence of the film involved Sharon and Billy in a helicopter above a volcano in Hawaii. We sent a camera crew and an experienced helicopter pilot over to the big island to shoot the background plates for the sequence, which we would later use on stage. I got a call informing me that while they were filming, the helicopter had mechanical problems and crashed deep into the inside of the volcano. The helicopter pilot had made a soft landing, so thankfully no one was hurt. He had radioed a distress signal. They waited near the chopper, but no one came. The cameraman, Mike Benson, and his assistant, Chris Duddy, decided to go separate ways to climb out of the volcano. Since the volcano was actively emitting smoke, visibility was limited and air quality was poor.

Very soon after Mike and Chris headed out on their own, another helicopter flew into the volcano and saved the pilot. However, because of the intense smoke inside the volcano, they could not locate Mike or Chris. Twenty-four hours later, with all of us back in LA monitoring every moment of the rescue mission, Chris climbed out of the top of the volcano. We were ecstatic but still wondering, where is Mike Benson?

As much as I wanted to, I couldn't go to Hawaii myself because my job was to keep the movie going. I sent my production manager Itsi Atkins to Hawaii to see what he could do. He spoke with naval air and rescue units who were doing everything they thought they could to find Mike, but they wouldn't send a chopper into the volcano. Itsi found a daredevil, an independent pilot who was willing to fly in to look for Mike.

Itsi was at the top of the volcano on a phone to me on the stage at Paramount. I put him on loudspeaker, so everyone on our set could hear. We had stopped shooting and were listening to the drama unfold. At least an hour went by with nothing. Then all of a sudden, Itsi said, "I think he's found something. There's something in the bucket dangling from the chopper! Don't know what it is but he's bringing it up. It's Mike! It's Mike! He's alive!" Cheers erupted all over the soundstage, and of course, we could practically hear them yelling all the way from Hawaii.

★ ★ ★

Our set photographer said she wanted to set me up with an actress friend of hers, Mary Crosby. When we met that winter, Mary and I clicked.

One of the things we had in common was that both our fathers were famous: hers—Bing Crosby—was internationally famous, while my dad was mainly known in Hollywood. Still, we could talk about what it was like to be the children of powerful men.

Mary was different than any other actress I'd known. Bigger than her love of acting was her love of nature. Living in nature was a necessity for her, and through her it began to be equally important to me. She lived on ten acres in the hills of Malibu, virtually in the middle of nowhere, with her three horses and her two dogs. I loved the adventure of driving to her house, riding horses with her, and especially running on the beach with her two labs.

Being immersed in the natural surroundings of her land and life-style had a positive and transformative effect on me. I realized how much I felt at home in nature and how meaningful it was for me to have animals in my life.

Mary had a second home in a remote part of Baja, on the Sea of Cortez, which we would visit together from time to time. She would spearfish while I—determined never to kill anything—snorkeled or swam among dolphins and vibrant schools of fish.

One day Mary and I were in her little fifteen-foot boat when suddenly a pod of orcas emerged out of the literal depths and came right up to our boat. I talked Mary out of jumping in to swim with them by convincing her they'd mistake her wetsuit for seal skin and might eat her.

She reluctantly conceded. The whales rolled and allowed us to pat their bellies right off the boat. We started the engines to see if they would follow us, which, to our delight, they all did. We stopped one more time, lost sight of them for a moment until all seven of them—from the biggest to the smallest—appeared again right off the bow of the boat. It was as if they came to say good-bye before they all dove down as one and went on their way.

The power and the unimaginable privilege of witnessing such a moment was not lost on me. I was aware of a feeling of deep calm, a satisfaction with my life just as it was, not as I hoped it would or could be someday.

★ ★ ★

I was soon working on another movie at Paramount. While there, I bought the rights to a book called *Losing Isaiah*, a powerful story about a young black woman addicted to crack, who abandons her baby in a dumpster. The child is found and taken to a hospital where a white volunteer nurse cares for him, develops a deep connection, and eventually takes him home so she and her husband can raise him.

When the baby, named Isaiah, is four or five years old, the birth mother has improved her life, is no longer an addict, and has located her child. She goes to court in an effort to get him back.

My friend Naomi Foner wrote the screenplay and her husband at the time, Steven Gyllenhaal, was attached to direct. (Yes, they are the parents of Jake and Maggie Gyllenhaal.)

We sent the draft to Paramount's production executives. On Monday morning I got a call from the head of production saying, "I'm sorry Howard, but we're never going to make a movie like this. It's a nice script but not gonna happen."

I was depressed because I thought it was a really good script. I called Naomi and Steve, and they stopped by to commiserate over lunch. We were sitting in my office, picking at our food, wondering if we should take it somewhere else because we knew it was too good not to get made. In that very moment of desperation, I got a call from Sherry Lansing, the head of the studio. Sherry said, "Hi, honey, isn't that a wonderful script? Who do you want to play the leads? Let's go. Let's make this movie." We were dumbfounded and thrilled.

Our first choice to play the volunteer nurse was Jessica Lange. At the time, Halle Berry was just coming up and was relatively unknown, but when she read for us, she blew us away. We had our leads and ultimately made what I thought was a damn good movie. I remember standing with Sherry Lansing in the back of a theater at a preview when she said, "Damn, I'm proud we made this film."

★ ★ ★

May 1994 was an auspicious month for the Koch family. Emily graduated from American University, and Billy married Kathy over Memorial Day weekend.

Melinda's husband, Alan, had done a lot of fund-raising for Clinton/Gore, who, once they got elected, nominated Alan to be the

US ambassador to Belgium. Once he was approved by the senate, he and Melinda moved to Belgium for what turned out to be the best adventure of their lives.

★ ★ ★

My friend Gary Lucchesi, now with a deal to produce exclusively for Paramount, had optioned the rights to the book *Primal Fear*, by William Diehl. He asked me if I would produce the film with him. We were going to hire Greg Hoblit as the director. I had met Greg several years before. I knew he hadn't directed a movie, but he had won eight Emmys for *Hill Street Blues, L.A. Law,* and *NYPD Blue.*

Richard Gere had committed to play the lead, but we needed another star to play the young boy at the center of the film. We thought that Sherry Lansing wouldn't make the film with only one star and an unknown actor for the second lead. We had already had several passes from well-known young stars and were holding our breath while waiting to hear from Leonardo DiCaprio.

Meanwhile, the head of Paramount's casting, Deb Aquila, had been scouring the nation for a great kid to play Aaron. She saw 2,500 young actors in New York alone. There were several she liked, but only one who her keen eye told her might be the one.

While still holding out for Leo, we decided to test two young actors, one from England and another from West Virginia (the one Deb saw in New York), who we were told had a stutter. When we met the latter, we weren't too concerned about his stutter because it seemed to come from nerves over the audition. Besides, his shyness seemed to fit the role of Aaron.

The character is arrested for allegedly murdering the monsignor in Chicago. As the story unfolds, we think that Aaron, a simple, stammering, sweet, and understated boy, suffers from split personality disorder. His other personality, Roy, is one tough mother who thinks Aaron is "a pussy" and is quite capable of murder.

Our young West Virginian actor was going to be the first of the two testing that day. Just before meeting him we'd gotten a disappointing call from Sherry that Leo had passed, so we were all a bit glum.

This kid walks on the stage and does several scenes with Richard. We liked what we saw, but we were especially eager to see the moment in the middle of the scene where Aaron changes into Roy. We were stunned by his transformation. He was so powerful he scared the crap out of all of us.

We looked at each other with a shared expression of "Holy shit, this kid can act!"

We showed the actor's test to Sherry, and while she thought he was very good, she wanted to do another one. We called and told him the first test was great, but he had to do one more. We took him to Sherry's office. She was sweet to him but said, "No pressure, honey, but the role is yours to lose."

We put the young actor through the wringer one more time. After Sherry viewed it, she had no choice but to allow Edward Norton, a virtual unknown, to play Aaron.

Edward recently told me about the experience of his audition. He said, "I had done a lot of them, but I hadn't gotten anything. When I went to meet with Deb Aquila, she actually got on the floor with me to read the scene. It changed everything because it was intimate and engaging in a way I'd never experienced before."

By the time we had cast him, we had learned that Edward was not the stuttering kid from West Virginia he had presented himself to be, but was in fact a patrician young man who had gone to Yale drama school. He had brilliantly fooled us all.

Those screen tests made the rounds of Hollywood, and before we even turned the motor on for the camera to begin filming *Primal Fear*, everyone in town had eyes on Edward Norton.

★ ★ ★

Coming back to my house late one night after a function, without any explanation Mary broke up with me. And just like that, she left. I was sucker punched. I was devastated.

The next morning on the set, Greg Hoblit, seeing what a wreck I was, put his arms around me and said, "You need help." Then he handed me the number of a therapist, who I saw that afternoon.

It was that crumbling version of myself who sat across the table from my old pal Gary Lucchesi, shortly before I turned fifty. I had run out of ways to escape looking at the deep hole I'd been digging—and ignoring—my whole life. No one can hide forever, and for me, the jig was finally up. I knew that what I had used to hold back the truth—finding another woman—had stopped working for me. My past had caught up with me and I knew I was going to need some spirituality if I was going to fill that hole.

Enter the rabbi.

36

One of the most significant days in my life—aside from the birth of my children—was the day I met Rabbi Jonathan Omer-man. I had been seeing a therapist and had found it helpful, but the rabbi introduced me to a depth of self-examination I had never experienced before.

Once I found myself sitting across from him in his humble and dimly lit office, I knew I was exactly where I belonged.

Imagine, I thought, this doesn't have a thing to do with meeting a new woman, with food I can eat too fast without tasting, or with producing another movie. This is about figuring out who I am as a man.

It suddenly occurred to me how overdue I was for this exploration.

I was able to tell him why I'd come, both because of the natural trust he engendered and because I had hit the lowest point of my life. I poured my heart out, telling him about my relationship problems with women and about what it was like to be the invisible junior to my beloved father's senior.

The rabbi listened without interruption, and when I had said everything I felt I had in me to say, we sat in a shared and sacred silence, allowing my words to encircle us. With that pause, he had done the equivalent of making room for me, and I felt not only the spaciousness of that generosity, but deeply understood.

After a few moments had passed, the rabbi broke the silence. He asked, "Who are you?"

"I'm a movie producer," I said.

"No, who are you?" he asked again.

"I'm a father and a son," I offered.

"C'mon, Howard. Who are you?"

I took a long time trying to find the answer.

"I'm a Jewish man," I said as if it had just dawned on me.

"Well, that's a start. What's your Hebrew name?"

I told him I didn't have one because my parents were not religious. Without hesitation, he said, "For your bar mitzvah, you will be given your own name."

He meant my Hebrew name, but when he said that, I broke down. At that moment I realized that for forty-nine years I'd carried my father's name.

I said to the rabbi with conviction, "I want my *own* name."

That's when he said the words that changed my life: "You can have it."

What? A rabbi said I could have my own name?

And that's how the process of being bar mitzvahed for my fiftieth birthday began.

The first thing we had to do was find *my* name. Rabbi Jonathan asked me what I wanted to be called. We discussed several possibilities, but something clicked for me when he wondered aloud if I'd ever had a nickname. I remembered that I used to write my initials, HWK, on the back of my school books, and a couple of kids had called me Hawk, though it never really stuck.

Interested, Rabbi Jonathan asked, "Do you know anything about hawks?"

"Well, they're birds of prey, I know that."

"Hawks mate for life," he said seriously.

I laughed self-consciously at the irony, telling him, "It's always what I wanted, but I haven't been very good at it."

Undeterred, he told me that hawks can also see from horizon to horizon at the same time and they have the ability to see a mouse from a half-mile away.

"Wouldn't it be wonderful," he asked, "if you could see the panoramic of your life and the detail all at the same time?"

"Yes, that would be wonderful, but isn't Hawk a pretentious name?"

His response, "Only if you allow it to be," was just one of many sobering and priceless words of wisdom the rabbi offered me over our time together.

A bar mitzvah is a Jewish ritual that marks the coming-of-age for a thirteen-year-old boy who will now be accountable for his actions. I may have been thirty-seven years late in coming to this moment, but I had arrived, and I was eager to take the step.

The rabbi and I continued to meet to discuss the practical matters of my bar mitzvah, as well as the symbolic significance of the journey I was embarking on. It was more than being responsible for myself; this was about accountability, aligning my inner and outer life. This was about how I was going to relate to that hole. Ritually changing my name in order to bring my authentic self into being meant that I had to separate from my father. I had to hand him back his name and give myself my own. I knew it would not be easy. I told the rabbi I'd give the name Hawk some serious consideration.

I decided to go away for a week to think deeply about my new name and what it would mean to get one. Obviously, this would be a major decision that would affect not only me but my children, my friends, and, not insignificantly, my parents, especially my father. I hoped that he might understand—not in terms of what I was doing *to* him, but in terms of what I was doing *for* myself.

I went to Telluride, Colorado. I swam, I hiked, and I thought. I spent my days pondering the name Hawk. I looked for signs and tried to follow my intuition.

One day while I walked down the main drag, I encountered a Native American man selling trinkets. I saw a piece that had a cloud, a lightning bolt, and the word "Listen" etched at the bottom. I was drawn to it, so I stopped to ask him what it meant.

He said, "Do you know how awake, aware, and attuned all our senses are in the moments between seeing the lightning and hearing the thunder—the way we listen so intently?"

"Yes, I know exactly what you mean," I assured him.

"Well, I made this piece as a reminder to stay awake and aware all the time, not just in the space between the lightning and the thunder. Do you see what I mean?"

Not only did I get what he meant, I bought that necklace, put it around my neck, and decided right there and then that I would be called Hawk; HWK for my initials, plus an "a" to represent an honest attempt to become awake and aware in all the moments of my life, not just the ones that are thundering.

I came back from Telluride, and the first person I called was Gary, excited to tell him my news.

"Hey, Gar, I want you to be the first to know that I *am* going to get bar mitzvahed for my fiftieth birthday!"

"That's great Howard. That's just great."

"Yeah, and I've decided to change my name too."

"What? You're kidding, right?" His voice was wavering.

"No, I'm not kidding. I'm changing my name for my bar mitzvah, and it's all because of you."

Gary said, in a tone that suggested he really didn't want to hear the answer, "Really? What are you changing your name to?"

"Hawk!"

"Hawk? Hawk what?" he asked incredulously.

"Just Hawk," I replied.

Gary, doing his best to hide his *OHMYGODYOU'VEGOTTO-BEKIDDING* voice, asked, "You mean like Cher?"

"Yeah. Like Cher. Only Hawk."

Silence. But this time, I didn't need to fill it in.

Over the years Gary's repeated the story, comfortable now that the years have passed, and fully willing to admit how concerned he was about that call. In fact, he said he was dying inside, sinking in Catholic guilt, wondering, "Dear God, what have I done? Howard wants to be called Hawk now! How is he ever gonna explain this one?"

Truthfully, I wasn't sure.

37

For the rest of the year leading up to my fiftieth, I spent one or two days a week talking with Rabbi Omer-man, deep in discussions about life, what it means to be Jewish, and the significance of my transition from Howard to Hawk.

The rabbi and I talked about the complexity of separating myself from my father by handing his name back to him and choosing my own at my bar mitzvah celebrating my fiftieth. These were mind-boggling days.

I was aware that although the discussions the rabbi and I were having were deeply meaningful to me, it wasn't the discipline that twelve-year-old boys traditionally experience when they prepare for their bar mitzvahs. I felt bad about that, and said to the rabbi one day, "I don't believe I deserve to get bar mitzvahed because, as opposed to learning Hebrew and reading the Torah, I'm just coming in and talking with you."

He didn't say anything immediately; by now I knew he was a take-a-pause-before-you-speak kind of man, but eventually, the rabbi asked if I knew the story of the man who jumped in the lake. I did not.

He said, "There was a man who saw a boy drowning in a lake. The man ran down to the pier and jumped right in. While in midair, he was thinking to himself, 'Am I jumping in the lake to save the boy, or am I jumping in the lake, to be a hero?'"

"Do you know the answer?" the rabbi asked.

"No," I admitted. "I don't."

"The answer is: he was jumping in the lake."

And then with his usual kindness, he added, "You're doing the work, Hawk. You deserve your bar mitzvah."

He called me Hawk! The chills that ran up my spine alerted me to the fact that this was my name now, and in this moment of being seen as Hawk, I knew it fit.

I was beginning to understand that my father—given his relationship to his father—had his own hole, and that hole had become part of his legacy to me. I began to understand that when my father stepped into the role of father himself, he had done the best he could, given his own wounds. Moving toward separating myself from him by changing my name had the effect of bringing me closer to him.

Another effect of being alone was realizing I wanted a dog.

I had rescued a wonderful dog for my parents from an organization called the Amanda Foundation. I called them to ask if they had any Labs available for adoption. They did—a Lab shepherd mix named Jennifer.

I said, "Instead of my coming to you to meet her, could you bring Jennifer to my home so I can see how we do together in my surroundings?"

It did not escape me that this was likely the first time I wanted a prospective female in my life to be able to adapt to me, not the other way around.

Two women from the foundation brought this shy dog, who was far more of a shepherd than a Lab, around the back gate of my house. As she stepped into my yard, she moved right into my heart.

I don't know if dogs can tiptoe, but Jennifer was so timid, her walk so slow and tentative, it seemed like she was doing exactly that. I got down on the ground, armed with treats, so she mustered up her courage, carefully slinked over to me, and took one. I learned she'd been abused by a man. I listened to her story while I petted her and fed her treats, trying to reassure her she'd be safe with me. She was gradually warming up to me, but I knew that no matter what, there was no way I'd be sending her back with the Amanda Foundation ladies.

When I told them as much, they said I should let them know if I changed my mind, but I assured them that wasn't going to happen.

When they left, I put a leash on Jennifer, and we took a little walk together in my neighborhood. While we walked, I talked to her, telling her I would never hurt her, and that she had a home now with me. I also told her I wasn't crazy about her name—or mine, for that matter—so we were both in for a change. I told her my name was going to be Hawk and hers, I decided, would be Pepper because she was all black. Maybe changing names wasn't so difficult after all.

Pepper and I hung out together that night, and she slept quietly in my bedroom in a crate I'd gotten after having been told it would make her feel secure.

The next day and every day after that when we could, we hiked together. Our regular spot was not far from my house. The land had a beautiful 360-degree view of downtown LA, the San Fernando Valley, and the Pacific Ocean. Pepper and I mostly had the place to ourselves, which left me plenty of time to think about my bar mitzvah and my new identity.

Mostly what was on my mind was how to tell my parents, especially my father. I visited them one weekend and we sat outside making small talk while I struggled with how to start. At some point, I said, "I have some news for you."

"Don't tell me you're getting married again," my mother said, sarcastically.

"No, nothing like that. But I've been giving some thought to my fiftieth birthday, and I've decided I'm going to get bar mitzvahed." Then I waited for a reaction.

My father was silent, but my mother asked, sincerely befuddled, "Why do you want to do that?"

"Well, to tell you the truth, I've been having a hard time lately, and I just thought I needed some spirituality in my life."

"That's great then, honey," Mom said supportively. "Right, Dad?"

"Sure," my dad chimed in, "go ahead and get yourself bar mitzva-hed." I wasn't sure by his response whether he actually cared or not, but I was pretty sure he'd care about what I had to say next.

"One more thing," I added hesitatingly. "I've decided to change my name too. I'm going to call myself Hawk. HWK for my initials and the added 'a' because I'm going to work on being awake and aware."

My mom reacted first. "What? Why are you doing that?" Dad was silent, letting my mother do the talking for both of them.

I tried to explain. "I don't know if you'll be able to understand, but let me tell you why. It's a privilege having Dad's name, but it's his name. All my life, when people hear my name, they immediately think of him, they talk about him, and I don't seem to exist at all. I don't intend any disrespect. I really don't. I just want my own name."

My mother was quiet, likely a bit stunned. Totally uncharacter-istically, she left; she got up and walked into the house. I could have counted on one hand the number of times in my life when my father and I had sat alone together. I'm not sure which one of us was more uncomfortable. I waited because I'd said what I had to say and had learned to be a bit more comfortable in the pause.

After what felt like an eternity my father said, "Howard is a great name. Why would you not want it?"

"Yeah, Dad, it is a great name. But it's your name; it's yours. I'm not you. I've been 'Little Howie' my whole life. I just can't be that anymore. I need a name of my own that allows me to be my own person. You're a hard act to follow, Dad. I really hope you'll try to understand."

As I recall, that was the end of our conversation. I left with mixed feelings. I was hugely relieved for having told them. I was disappointed because I had held out hope that he might say something like, "I under-stand. It must have been hard carrying my name all these years. I'm proud of you for doing this." If I'm honest with myself, I may have been disappointed in his reaction, but I was not surprised.

My father was seventy-nine at the time, and I did not want to hurt him. At the same time, I felt strong and, truthfully, proud of myself, because I hadn't come to ask for permission; I'd come to tell him about my decision, and that's what I'd done.

I told my children shortly after, knowing that with everything else I'd put them through, here was another crazy thing their dad was doing that they would have to contend with. They reacted with their usual mix of raised eyebrows, jokes, and gracious acceptance.

Then I started telling friends. At one point I called a woman I knew, Harley Jane Kozak, who had changed her name when she was only eighteen. I was curious how she'd told everybody. Harley said she'd written a letter to her friends, an idea that I loved and latched onto. This is the one I wrote:

August 1995

Dear Family and Friends,

As most of you know, I've been going through a lot of personal changes, and in December I will celebrate birthday #50!

With the help of some very good old friends, and a few amazing new ones, I have been open enough to receive some wonderful gifts. Among these gifts are some ideas that I have latched onto and made my own, two of which I would like to share with you.

Firstly, for my fiftieth birthday I'm going to have my own bar mitzvah—no, I didn't have one when I was thirteen (my choice). I'll fill you in with more details later, but please save the date: Thursday, December 14th, 1995.

Secondly, I've never loved Howie, or Junior, so I've decided to give myself my own name. It's "HAWK," my initials, H.W.K., plus an "A" for "aware" and "awake" (which I'm working to become).

Try it out loud, "Hawk."

Smile and say it, "Hawk."

Not Hawk Koch. That sounds like focaccia, the Italian bread! Just "Hawk."

Now try these simple phrases:

"Hi, Hawk."

"Como estas, Hawk?"

"Hawk, let's have dinner."

Now try talking about me behind my back. "Did you notice how much more focused Hawk is becoming? He listens!"

For business, credits, banking, taxes, et al., I'm still and will always be—Howard W. Koch, Jr.

Hawk, messenger of the sky, circle my dreams and teach me the message as we fly.

Thank you for your friendship and the energy you've expended with me.

Love,

Shalom,

Namaste

The letter went out, and the reactions were—well, mixed at best. The people who embraced it wanted to know more, and so they leaned into me with genuine curiosity. Some understood that I was going through a cathartic change and were there for me. Others couldn't handle it and told me they'd never call me Hawk. Some laughed it off and thought it was silly. No matter what, I continued to move ahead.

Not knowing anything about how to produce a bar mitzvah, I asked the rabbi if I needed to have it in a temple.

"No, have it wherever you want, and then have a party, just like kids do when they're thirteen."

I decided to have it at Michael's in Santa Monica. I'd known the owner, Michael McCarty, for a long time and wanted to celebrate somewhere I felt safe. The restaurant's outdoor patio was, and still is, absolutely beautiful. He closed the restaurant for me. The chairs on the back patio were to be set up auditorium style, and we'd put a table at the back to hold the Torah and whatever else was needed for the ceremony. Afterward, we'd go inside for a toast and breaking of the bread, while Michael's staff rearranged the back patio tables for dinner. My friend Tim Sexton found a great band so that we could eat, sing, and dance the night away, celebrating this auspicious Jewish rite of passage.

December 14, 1995, I was reborn—fifty years to the day after my birth. I had prepared my Torah portion in English and had worked on my speech for some time. I had invited approximately a hundred people to join me. I greeted everyone, looking each of them directly in the eye and thanking them for coming and being there for me. Once everyone had arrived, we went in to begin the ceremony. Rabbi Omer-man gave me a nod, my cue to walk up to the front of the bimah. In order to bring myself fully into this sacred moment, I repeated what had by then become my personal mantra: magic time.

Traditionally the grandfather gives the Torah to the father, who then hands it to his thirteen-year-old son. In my case, my three children gave it to me. My father and mother sat in the first row with my sister and brother-in-law, my friends filling in the rest of the seats.

I had written a speech that I had gone over many times. I wanted everyone to understand exactly what taking this step meant to me. I shared a story from the Torah about Jacob, whose name was changed to Israel as evidence of his own spiritual affirmation. I learned that in language theory, a thing is not considered to exist until it is named. In this way, I was bringing myself into existence.

Reading the speech and looking around at my family and friends, I allowed myself to feel the import of the moment fully.

After the ceremony and the wonderful dinner in Michael's garden, I loved dancing with everyone who came to celebrate one of the most important days of my life. Just like I did all those years before at the Ad-Lib in London when I danced with Nedra Talley, I let go.

As if all this wasn't enough to send one man over the moon, the final gift of the night came when my son Billy and his wife, Kathy, announced they were having a baby. Not only was this night the night I stepped into a new identity, to my great delight, that identity was going to include being a grandfather.

We would learn a few months later that Billy and Kathy weren't just adding one new Koch to the family; they were having twins!

Celebrating *Nothing in Common* with Garry Marshall and Tom Hanks.
NOTHING IN COMMON © 1986 TriStar Pictures, Inc. All Rights Reserved.
Courtesy of TriStar Pictures.

With Francis Coppola on the set of *Peggy Sue Got Married*. PEGGY SUE GOT
MARRIED © 1986 TriStar Pictures, Inc. All Rights Reserved. Courtesy of
TriStar Pictures.

The *Wayne's World* Cast—PARTY ON! © Paramount Pictures Corp.
All Rights Reserved.

Wayne's World set visit with Billy Koch, Mike Myers, Robert Patrick, Robby
Koch, and me. © Paramount Pictures Corp. All Rights Reserved.

Screening of *Virtuosity* with Gary Lucchesi, Sherry Lansing, and Denzel Washington. © Paramount Pictures Corp. All Rights Reserved.

A happy day on *Primal Fear* with Michael Chapman, Richard Gere, Laura Linney, Hawk, Edward Norton, and (back) Alfre Woodard. © Paramount Pictures Corp. All Rights Reserved.

With Rabbi Omer-Man and my children at my Bar Mitzvah.

My Bar Mitzvah with Helen Mirren, Taylor Hackford, and my father.

My Bar Mitzvah with my parents.

My Bar Mitzvah with David Field and Gary Lucchesi.

On the set of *Keeping the Faith* with Ben Stiller, Ron Rifkin, Miloš Forman, Edward Norton, Eli Wallach, and me. © Touchstone Pictures. Photo by Glen Wilson.

Opening remarks at the 85th Academy Awards Nominee Luncheon. Copyright © Academy of Motion Picture Arts and Sciences.

Fun with Ryan Gosling on *Fracture*. Licensed by: Warner Bros. Entertainment, Inc. All Rights Reserved.

Nominees Luncheon 2013 with Quvenzhané Wallis and all the other nominees. Copyright © Academy of Motion Picture Arts and Sciences.

Governor's Ball with Barbra, Adele, and Shirley Bassey. © Alex J. Berliner/ ABImages.

My kids, Robby, Emily, and Billy Koch, at Robby's fortieth birthday party.

My grandsons Payton, Walker, Teddy, Charlie, and Cooper Koch.

Molly and Hawk at the beach.

38

After my bar mitzvah, I began to experience myself as Hawk and tried to help those in my personal life and my professional life to do the same. I noticed that when I met people for the first time, even if they knew my dad, they tended to talk *to* me, often bypassing a conversation about my father. I was an individual first to them, and I liked how that made me feel.

I continued to walk with Pepper nearly every day up into the hills of Benedict Canyon. I dated a bit, but I wasn't looking for a partnership anymore. After all, I had one with Pepper, and better still, I was beginning to have one with myself. My focus was on finishing post on *Primal Fear* and prepping, and then starting to shoot a new movie for Paramount, *The Beautician and the Beast.* I was truly happy.

Adding to that happiness was the birth, on July 16, 1996, of my two grandsons, Cooper and Payton Koch. To be a grandfather to these two beautiful boys from this burgeoning, more awake place in myself was an incredible gift. For the first time that I could remember, the furthest thing from my mind was meeting a woman. And wouldn't you know...

On Friday, July 26, 1996, just ten days after the twins were born, I had a shooting call at ten in the morning, which meant I could get in an early hike with Pepper on our mountaintop before driving into work.

It was gorgeous out, and as usual, we had the place to ourselves. Pepper didn't need a leash anymore, so she was a bit ahead of me sniffing all the bushes along the way. I noticed the yellow lab and the black mutt running toward us and was surprised that Pepper, who was known to growl (but never bite) at other dogs, didn't this time. She greeted these two like long-lost friends. Relaxed now that the dog energy was friendly, I noticed the woman with the dogs. She wore a white tank top, shorts, and hiking boots, no makeup. She had a friendly smile. There was something about her I liked immediately.

When she told me her name was Molly, I realized I liked her name as well as her voice. Since our dogs were still communing, I asked her if she wanted to keep going and was happy when she agreed. I found out she was preparing for her written and oral exams to become a marriage and family therapist. We must have walked and talked for an hour or so, during which time I was wondering if it would be presumptuous of me to ask her out—after all, we'd only just met. Since we'd been talking about how much we loved hiking with our dogs, I mustered up my courage and said, "You know, next Tuesday is a full moon. Do you want to meet up here with the dogs and hike in the evening?" She pondered my question for just long enough to convince me she was about to say no, so I was surprised when she said yes instead.

I had to memorize her number because neither of us had paper or pen. There were two ways into this hiking area, and since we'd each taken a different route, I was going to have to remember her number for quite some time. I repeated it over and over in my head until I got home and could write it down.

I showered, got dressed for work, and, as I was heading in, decided to call her to ask, "Why are we waiting until next Tuesday night? Why don't we go out tomorrow?" I was disappointed when she told me she had plans. I thanked her, said I was looking forward to Tuesday, and then I let it go, figuring she had a boyfriend or at least wasn't as available as I'd hoped. Clearly, I was doing the Joe's Service Station–flat tire story again—filling in the blanks before I knew any of the details.

But not too long after we'd hung up, Molly called back to say that she was going to her friend's fiftieth birthday party on Saturday night. She asked if I wanted to join her. I did.

I picked her up that Saturday night at a cute little house on a narrow street in Benedict Canyon. Mind you, by this time in my life—at fifty years old—I had certainly knocked on a lot of doors for a first date, but for some reason, this felt different. As I knocked, I could see her shadow through the window, running around getting ready. She came to the door looking quite a bit different than she did wearing the tank top, shorts, and boots. When she got dressed up, all I can say is, as beautiful as she was that Friday morning, Saturday night she looked incredible.

We drove to her friend's house, she introduced me to a few people, but before too long we found ourselves sitting alone and talking. And that's where we remained the rest of the night. That's when I learned why Molly was up on that mountaintop. I was stunned to learn that the day we met, July 26, was the two-year anniversary of her late-husband's death. I had no idea she was a young widow who had hiked up with her dogs that morning to do a ritual on the top of the mountain to say a final good-bye to him. When she got to the top, she acknowledged her intention to move on with her life. Just moments after she did, she walked down the hill with her dogs and ran into Pepper and me.

She told me she realized that the "no thank you" she had planned to tell me after I invited her out seemed so insignificant in comparison to the enormity of meeting someone in that very moment, that she forced herself to say yes instead. She said yes to life, and I was really glad she did.

When Tuesday finally rolled around, we took our dogs back up to that magical mountain and continued to talk and walk. At one point I made a huge mistake by trying to kiss her. Her reaction made me realize I was moving way too fast. I busted myself realizing that "fast" was Howard's way. As Hawk, I needed to slow down to honor her and also to acknowledge the part of me who was working hard to be awake and aware.

I learned as we continued to see one another that there were lots of ways in which Molly was different than anyone I had ever dated. She had a calmness about her that helped me to slow down, to take time to think and reflect.

Molly seemed to understand who my father was without going into a swoon about how much she adored him, unlike a lot of women I dated.

She came from an entertainment background herself. Her grandparents were the iconic radio couple Fibber McGee and Molly. Since her mother was a stage, film, and TV actress, and her father was a live television director, Molly knew firsthand about the industry.

For the next two weeks, we went out a lot and talked all the time. Just before I was about to leave for filming in Prague, I went to visit her at her home, mainly to say good-bye. I was sitting on a chair outside on her deck, and she was sitting across from me. I had not come close to her the entire two weeks. At the end of our visit, Molly got up from her chair and said, "Don't move. Don't do a thing. Just sit there." I felt scared. *Whoa*, I thought. I wasn't comfortable not being the one in control. I didn't move. She walked over to where I was sitting, leaned down, and planted the best kiss I've ever had on my lips. "Have a safe trip. I'll see you when you get back."

Oh, my God, now what do I do? I wondered. I'm in trouble here.

While I was filming in Prague, I got a call from Billy. At the time, he, Kathy, their infant twins, Payton and Cooper, and their three Labradors lived just three doors away from the Museum of Tolerance. Billy sounded upset when he said, "There's a bomb threat at the museum, and we've been told we have to evacuate immediately. Can we come up to your house?"

"Yes, of course, move in and stay there as long as you need to." Being displaced with two infants, I know it was difficult for them, but I have to say, when I got home, I loved every minute of them being there, especially since I could be close to the babies, who were still only weeks old.

I started to see Molly right after my return. She told me that while I was away, she'd gotten calls from a few people who warned her about me. "He's fun to be around," they said, "but not to get serious about. Don't get hurt." I really needed to let her know I'd changed.

I was taking her to a Dodger game one night to meet some friends of mine. On the way to the stadium, I reassured her. "There's no pressure. I'm not looking to sleep with you or even kiss you. Let's just see how it goes as friends. Let's just see where our relationship goes." I could see that made Molly feel much more comfortable.

Since Molly never knew me as Howard, it was completely natural for her to call me Hawk. I grew more comfortable in my name just knowing her.

One night she came over to have dinner with Billy's family and me. I wanted them to get to know one another. We had ordered food so we could eat at home, letting all the dogs play and the twins sleep. As Molly was leaving, she said something polite to Billy along the lines of "It was great meeting you. I look forward to seeing you next time." Molly was not just taken aback but crushed when Billy said, "It was nice meeting you too, but I know my dad. I might not be seeing you again."

I knew where that came from in him. Billy's not the least bit confrontational, but his comment clearly revealed how deeply he'd been affected by my serial dating. It broke my heart.

Billy's prediction could not have been more wrong. This time, my past was not to be my prologue. Molly and I started seeing each other all the time.

I finished *Beautician* and gave a prerelease party at my house for *Primal Fear.* I could see there was a difference in the way people looked at Molly, compared to how they looked at any other woman I had been with. Uh-oh, I couldn't believe I was getting serious.

I asked Molly to come with me to meet my therapist, the guy I had been seeing ever since Mary had broken up with me. At some point during the appointment, my therapist turned to Molly and asked, "What would you like out of this relationship?" Molly thought a minute (she pauses too) and then answered, "I think I'd like to spend the rest of my life with Hawk." Lucky, I didn't have food in my mouth because it would have shot out of it like water from a fire hose.

When the therapist asked me the same question, I said that up until now, I had been certain I was the guy who was never getting married again. Not ever. Except, in this case, I was also certain that this was the woman I was supposed to spend the rest of my life with.

On January 3, 1998, in front of a small group of friends and family, Molly and I were married. The two of us and our dogs stood inside a sacred circle made of white roses. Our wrists were bound with an old Irish scarf belonging to Molly's grandmother, to symbolize the knot we tied that day. It was a beautiful ceremony followed by dancing and an incredible dinner made by Wolfgang Puck, who I'd known since the early days at Spago. We had hired Wolfgang's crew to cook our dinner, but I didn't know until I walked into their makeshift kitchen in our garage that Wolfgang had come to cook the meal himself. What a night.

39

It wasn't long before we were settled into our shared life. Since I had become Hawk, people who knew me well told me they saw a difference in me. Maybe I was more consciously awake and aware. Molly, having become a Jungian analyst, had a way of asking questions that made me think more deeply about things.

The fact that she came from an entertainment background meant she understood my business and my passion for it, but at the same time knew it for what it was. She couldn't have cared less about celebrities, and that made me able to trust her more than I had trusted anyone else in my life. If Molly could have a real interaction with someone on a human level, that's what was interesting to her. I think people see that genuineness in Molly. My grandkids sure did. I can't tell you how many times they'd come over and say, "Oh, hi, Grandpa. Where's Molly?" There is something special about her, and anybody who gets to know her says to me, "A blind squirrel found an acorn." That's how I felt.

While it was becoming harder to get movies made at Paramount, I was lucky enough to be developing two projects outside of the studio. While Edward Norton and I were making *Primal Fear* and becoming friends, he had introduced me to his best friend, Stuart Blumberg. While working on *Primal*, Edward asked me to read and comment on an early version of Stuart's script, *Keeping the Faith*. I continued to read and comment on various drafts until it was ready to be submitted to potential buyers, by which time Edward had asked me to produce it.

I first met Toby Emmerich when I sat next to him at a bar mitzvah (not mine). We didn't have to talk for too long for me to see that Toby was whip-smart and extremely talented. At the time he was head of music at New Line Cinema. We hit it off, and he told me about a script he'd written called *Frequency*.

When I asked if I could read it, he said, "Sure, and by the way, if you can get a director of note on board, you can produce it."

I read the script, loved it, and called Toby, asking, "How would you feel about Greg Hoblit? This is right up his alley. He loves sports, and he loves the spiritual stuff." (*Frequency* is the beautiful and powerful story of an accidental radio link that connects a son with his father who had died thirty years earlier.) Toby and everyone else at New Line were excited about the possibility of having Greg direct *Frequency*. I reached Greg at a car dealership in the valley.

I said, "Hey, you gotta read this script *Frequency*," and he said, "Oh yeah, I've got it."

That was typical Greg. And my response to him was pretty typical of me too: "Well, read it for God's sake. Don't just get it and let it sit on your desk. Read the fucking thing, will ya?"

Greg called me the next day and told me he loved it. We scheduled a meeting with Toby and Bob Shaye, the chairman and founder of New Line, who made a deal with us to move forward.

Amy Pascal at Sony picked up *Keeping the Faith,* and we started developing it there. Eventually, Sony put it in turnaround, at which point Spyglass Entertainment picked it up, and I was on my way with that one. The problem was that we were also on our way with *Frequency*, and there was no way to be in two places at once.

Congratulations and condolences were definitely in order because both movies ended up prepping and shooting concurrently, *Frequency* in Toronto, and *Keeping the Faith* in New York City. It was a situation designed to disappoint someone, including me, since I pride myself on being on set all the time.

Since this was going to be Edward's directing debut, I spent more time on set with him than I did with Greg on *Frequency,* a fact that I'll always feel bad about. Fortunately, Greg, Toby, Edward, and Stuart are still my friends, and both movies remain projects I'm proud of.

That was the good news. The bad news was that I would soon find out that Paramount, my home for the last ten years, had decided to let me go. I'm so grateful to the various studio gods who kept me there for as long as they did.

40

Before filming began for *Keeping the Faith* and *Frequency*, our whole family began noticing that my dad's memory was becoming increasingly impaired. At eighty-three years old, he was still working out of his Paramount office and his long-time secretary, Laurie Abdo, had been filling in the blanks for him—a kindness that until now had left us unaware of just how profoundly bad it had gotten. When it was time to renew his driver's license, we were worried that maybe he shouldn't be driving anymore.

Living in the sprawl of Southern California, freedom and independence are defined by being able to drive yourself anywhere, anytime. I was praying Dad would not lose this privilege, knowing how it would shatter him if he did.

I'd heard about a place where you could have an elderly person's mental stability checked before their DMV test. I made an appointment, picked up my dad, and drove him to the examination. Dad was perfectly willing to go because he thought it was a tutoring session before the actual DMV. For a moment, I too allowed myself to believe that was true.

We were met downstairs by a very nice lady, who after introducing herself, told my dad, "Okay, Mr. Koch, we're just going to do a few tests."

"Sure, sweetheart, let's you and I do this," he said with his usual kindness.

There was a piece of paper with a circle on it, like a clock, except at the top was the number one. The number two was at the bottom, three was to the left—and four, five, six, seven, and eight were scattered randomly around the edge of the circle. Handing my dad a pencil, she said, "Okay, find the number one and draw a line from it to number two and then three and four, and so on through number eight."

My dad put his pencil on the circle and waited a beat. Then another and another beat until it became clear that he didn't have a clue where to start. My father was unable to find number one.

Oh, my God, what is going on? I thought, beginning to panic. I kept my eyes down until I regained a bit of composure.

My dad failed every test he was given. When I finally made eye contact with the woman, she looked at me with compassion, as if to say, "Yes, we know about these things."

We drove back with a tense silence between us the size of Texas. It was as if some truth that had been there for quite some time suddenly revealed its full extent. One of the reasons my father had been so beloved was because he always remembered the name of every crew member, parking attendant, and waitress. I was trying to reconcile the man who had been so huge and powerful to everyone—myself included—with this new image of him losing his memory as he got increasingly smaller and more dependent.

What that meant to me emotionally began to get eclipsed by the knowledge that like my father's life, my life was going to change drastically as well. I had never thought about stepping into his place. You don't step *into* the place of a man like that. You strengthen yourself so you can step *up* instead.

I made an appointment with a gerontologist. My mom and I took Dad to meet him. When the doctor asked some questions that my dad could not answer, it was yet another confirmation that he had more problems than we had allowed ourselves to believe. Till that point, denial had been our friend, but that day it stormed out and slammed the door.

Dad's life began to change in significant ways that made him really angry at me. For starters, I was the one who had to take away his car keys, an action I would not recommend for any son. We should have let a doctor do it. We were fortunate enough to be able to afford to get him a driver, but that annoyed him even more because it underscored the fact that he would never drive again. No matter what was going on with him mentally, he knew he wanted to retain control of his life, and it was heartbreaking to witness him losing that option.

Meanwhile, the rest of my life had to—and did—go on. Chuck Fries, the renowned television producer, asked me to meet with him. He told me he was running for president of the Producers Guild of America and wanted me to join as well and then run for vice president, because as he said, "I think we could do a lot of good for producers."

I thought about it a lot. I had been a member of the Directors Guild since 1968 and had been on many committees at the Academy. I had never considered becoming a member of the PGA because it didn't have any weight in the industry. But since producers had lost more and more respect in Hollywood, I thought Chuck's suggestion would be a really good opportunity for me to work for our collective rights, and hopefully begin to make the guild effective.

The sequence in which credits are displayed in films and on television, both on-screen and in advertising, is highly negotiated, emotionally fraught, and frequently an expression of ego. It had gotten so bad for producers that the new contract negotiated between the six major studios and the Writers Guild of America gave the writers the last credit on-screen and in paid ads, before the director credit. This was a huge blow to producers, whose credit had always been listed just before the director credit.

I decided to run and was elected as vice president, but Chuck Fries lost to Thom Mount. Thom and I got along well and started to work together on regaining respect for producers and the whole producing team.

Producers had lost even more respect by 1998 when *Shakespeare in Love* won the Oscar for best picture and five producers came up to accept it. The producer has always been awarded the Oscar for best picture. Over the years it's always been one or two producers. When five won, it was an embarrassment to our profession. Everyone said, "Wait a minute, if it took five producers to make this movie, something is really wrong!" The Academy, equally embarrassed, instituted a rule shortly after that stipulating no more than three producers could take home the Oscar.

We had to do something to restore our reputations and protect our rights. In order to do that, it was clear that we needed more influential producers to get involved, and more PGA members overall. I started making calls to all the producers I knew, saying, "If you want to have a platform to try and restore respect for the producer, you have to join our guild." I'm proud to say I got about 150 of the top producers in town to join by speaking to each one individually. That's a lot of calls, even for a talker like me.

When it came time to look for a new president, we felt we needed someone with real clout. Kathy Kennedy, whose films included *E.T.*, *Jurassic Park*, and *The Sixth Sense*, was—and still is—one of the top producers in Hollywood. She was Spielberg's producer, and if we could get her to join us, the guild would take on a whole new gravitas. When she agreed to accept the mantle, things really began to change.

We merged with the American Association of Producers and, in doing so, added more than eight hundred new members.

Meanwhile, we had begun to put our heads together to define what a producer does. We wanted to ensure that only people who did the actual work of producing a movie would be eligible to receive the Producers Guild Award and the Academy Award. Part of what began to erode the reputations of producers was the fact that producing credits became negotiable, meaning that just about anyone could have a producer credit if they knew the right person or put in the right amount of money.

At one point, a group of us from the PGA went to Kathy's house for a retreat to brainstorm on this issue. There was no confusion about what a director, an actor, or a writer did, but producing was a different animal altogether. There were lots of functions that fell under the umbrella of producing, even though not every producer was involved in all of them.

Kathy proposed that we should establish a set of criteria in order to know what a producer does. So we sat in a room and discussed what we thought constituted the work of a producer. From that, we gathered more than forty-five points setting forth what a producer does, from finding the material, developing it, getting the financing, overseeing preproduction, production, post-production, all the way to marketing and distribution. If you do a majority of those functions, then you're credited as a producer and eligible for the Producers Guild Award for best picture. We hoped eventually to get the Academy to go along with us by adhering to our criteria.

We decided to put this code of credits together for our award. The Producers Guild would arbitrate relevant movies and ultimately give the award to the people or the person who actually fulfilled those criteria. That resulted in a lot more people joining the guild, so that before too long, our membership went from approximately 1,800 to the more than 8,500 we have today. I'm extremely proud of my role in that growth.

In 2000, Charles Fitzsimons, who had been executive director of the PGA since its inception, retired. To our good fortune, an executive search led us to Vance Van Petten, and nineteen years later he is still the heart and soul of our guild.

★ ★ ★

My father was declining. We did some investigating and searched for help. We knew that Frank Sinatra had suffered from dementia and Alzheimer's, so we found and met with the doctor who had cared for him, Randall Espinoza, a geriatric psychiatrist at UCLA.

Dr. Espinoza met with Dad, and we were both relieved and scared when he knew exactly what was going on and what we could expect to happen. From that point on, Dr. Espinoza met with us once a week. He'd come out to the house and sit with us, and he'd ask my dad how he was doing, assessing the progression of his disease. I'd walk the doctor out to his car, and he'd tell me what we should expect each week. Dr. Espinoza's help was immeasurable.

Dad's illness progressed as we were told to expect, and he continued to decline. Not only was he losing his memory, but he was often angry—another typical symptom, but one that none of us were used to experiencing from my dad, who had always been the picture of composure and "the nicest man in the world."

At some point along the trajectory of Dad's illness, the Motion Picture & Television Fund called to say they wanted to honor him with a Golden Boot at The Golden Boot Awards, their annual fund-raising dinner. The awards evening honors actors, actresses, and crew members who've made significant contributions to the Western genre in both movies and television. God knows, my dad had made enough Westerns in his life to have earned it; it's just that by now he was confused most days and I didn't think he could handle it.

The fund was established in 1921 by Mary Pickford and Douglas Fairbanks in order to care for actors in need of either financial or medical support. Today the fund has a sprawling campus in Woodland Hills with residents who represent a cross-section of the motion picture and television industries. We have independent and assisted-living, long-term care, and an Alzheimer's wing. And we continue to give financial aid and health care to more than a hundred thousand industry members. It's a wonderful charity.

I had told the fund it was really great they wanted to give him the award, but I wasn't sure he could get up and say something in front of 1,200 people in the big ballroom at the Beverly Hilton. Still, Mom and I decided we should go ahead and give it a try, that it would make Dad happy.

I told Dad he was going to get the award. On a good day, he'd remember, but most of the time he forgot. The day of the dinner we got him all dressed up, black tie, and Molly, my mother, and I drove him to the Hilton. I was nervous, wondering what was going to happen when he got up to accept the award.

A few minutes before it was his turn, the stage manager came to escort us backstage. Looking at my dad, I could tell he had no idea what was going on. I remember the sinking feeling in my stomach when I heard the presenter say, "Let's hear it for Howard W. Koch."

At that moment I took hold of my dad's arm to accompany him onstage, but he suddenly and forcefully pushed me away. He literally elbowed me, as if to say, "Get out of my way. This is *my* moment!" And then he walked onto that stage and dazzled everyone with a wonderful—and perfectly lucid—acceptance speech. I learned later that with Alzheimer's, the ego is often the last to go. That was certainly true in my dad's case.

Naturally, everyone at the fund looked at me afterward like I was the one in serious mental decline. At the end of the night, we were all in the car and Dad was sitting shotgun holding his award while I drove and Molly and Mom sat in the back seat. At one point he looked down at the golden boot in his lap, turned to me in utter confusion, and demanded to know, "What the hell is this?"

"You were given a great honor, Dad, and you deserved it." He smiled as his eyes glazed over with absolutely no understanding whatsoever.

During this troubling time there was some good news. Billy's wife, Kathy, gave birth to our third grandson, Walker Koch.

41

I had to go to Mexico to shoot a portion of *Collateral Damage*. Because I couldn't be at the weekly meetings with Dr. Espinoza, we scheduled phone conferences with him and my whole family, but being on a conference call from Mexico made me feel ineffective and added to the stress.

We finished shooting in Mexico and came back to LA to film. Dad had gotten so bad that it was time to bring in hospice. By now he'd forgotten how to eat, and rather than take any drastic measures, they put him on morphine to ensure he'd be comfortable. We knew he didn't have much longer to live.

One evening we were in the entertainment room downstairs at my parents' house. My dad was there in his hospital bed, in a coma, with all the family gathered. Billy suggested that we put on the music he loved. We told stories about him as we all listened to Sinatra singing the songs that underscored my father's life. We didn't know if he could hear us, but we talked to him late into the night as if he could. Finally, we all went home.

Melinda, who'd been staying with Mom at the house, called very early the next morning to let me know that Dad was gone. Molly and I jumped in the car and went to the house, where I became aware of the strangest feeling I'd ever felt. When I walked into the room, he had been gone less than fifteen minutes. I felt his presence, and at the same time, I was hit with the knowledge that the legend was gone. And so was my dad.

I felt all the years melt away into the love I had for this man who I really never knew and who never knew me. Grief came, but the moment it did, so did the realization that there was work to be done, and since I felt the burden of it, I jumped right in. Work was easier to deal with than grief.

He didn't want a funeral—Dad wanted to have his ashes spread over Turkey Crossing in Kanab, Utah, where he had made all his B western movies with his partner, Aubrey Schenck.

In work mode now, I began to plan a memorial service. Sherry Lansing and Alison Jackson, events coordinator at Paramount where my dad had been for thirty-eight years, allowed us to use the new Paramount Theatre for the memorial.

While the service was being planned, we'd gotten the ashes back and had made arrangements to fly up to Kanab, Utah. My friend George Schenck, Aubrey's son, told me he still had his dad's ashes and said, "Why don't we go up there together?"

That made perfect sense.

A friend of the family had a four-seater plane—just enough room to accommodate George, myself, Melinda, and my mom. He offered to pick us up and fly us to Utah. We flew up to Kanab where I had made arrangements for a single-engine plane to meet us there and fly us over Turkey Crossing. We were met and hosted by the city fathers of this wonderful little town, who knew how much my dad and Aubrey had contributed in the '50s and '60s to making Kanab the "little Hollywood of Utah."

We got in the plane—Melinda and Mom in the front and George and I on either side in the back. The pilot told us he would cue us when it was time to open the windows and release the ashes, and that at that moment he would tip the wing. Roger that. We flew up, and he cued us and tipped the wing, at which point we opened our windows and scattered the ashes of our fathers. We were not prepared for the wind that came up at that very moment, and blew those ashes right back in the window, covering George and me in our fathers' dust. It was like a scene from a bad horror movie. Wiping ash from our mouths and sputtering, we couldn't help but wonder if our dads had orchestrated their last joke on their grieving sons. "Always leave 'em laughing," we could practically hear them saying.

Back on the ground now, a huge V formation of Canadian Geese honked over our heads as they flew toward Turkey Crossing. George and I made a joke that that was Aubrey and Dad again, this time waving a final good-bye.

The astonished city fathers told us, "You don't know how strange that is, because we don't have Canadian Geese this time of year."

That left us all deeply touched and in awe of the mystery that comes with straddling that place between life and death.

We flew back and had the memorial service on a rainy Sunday.

My father loved the horses and the race track, so it made sense to have the service start with the bugler from Hollywood Park playing "First Call," the tune that brings the thoroughbreds to the post.

A lot of people attended; the theater was packed, as was the lobby. We put folding chairs and television monitors in the lobby so people could hear and see the speakers. The number of people who showed up was a testament to how beloved my father was. Having found my peace with the limitations of our relationship, what remained was my love for him and my gratitude for everything he did for me.

In the end, I felt like I, Hawk Koch, gave my dad, Howard W. Koch, a great and honorable send-off. To this day, I still think it's the best thing I've ever produced.

42

I was not prepared for what it would be like to lose my father. Despite knowing it would happen, I was not prepared for how deeply I would feel his loss. Because of his generosity and loyalty to family, I had an all-access pass to his professional life.

I had been hearing my entire life that I looked exactly like my father. Ever since his passing, I can look in the mirror and see his face staring back at me. In those moments, I catch my breath and think, *Oh, my God, it's him.* Sometimes I hear his voice. There are still moments when I hear myself saying something he would have said. It's eerie, sometimes uncomfortable, but when I allow myself the full experience of it, I feel a warm embrace, like the hug I could never elicit from him when he was alive.

From the moment of his death, I became the patriarch of our family, pretty much as my father asked me to do when he thought he might die all those years earlier at the Mayo Clinic.

My new role included taking care of my mother, who was beside herself with grief. It's understandable given that from the time she was a teenager, she was a planet orbiting the sun of my dad, the center of her universe. She tried to live her life as best she could without him, but the truth was, she was never really happy again.

She rumbled around alone in the house on Crescent Drive where they had lived for forty years, but two years after Dad died, we sold their home and Mom moved into a condominium. The newness of that soon wore off, and she became increasingly lonely. Added to that were occasional bouts of lung problems, meaning she had to be taken to UCLA emergency.

Because I was on the board of the Motion Picture & Television Fund, I knew just how great a place the home and the community it fosters was, so I suggested that we go out together and take a look at it as a possible place for her to move. Despite her initial resistance, when I took her to lunch at the home's cafe and she reconnected with people she'd known her whole life who were also living there, she began to change her mind. We showed her a studio apartment, explained all the social activities that would be available to her, and before too long she made the move, fully enjoying swimming, walking, watching movies, and interacting socially. It took a lot of stress off of my sister and me.

But the upswing in the quality of her life was only temporary, and by 2008 her health was in decline. My mother, Ruth Koch, passed away peacefully at the Motion Picture & Television home on February 28, 2009. She was eighty-nine.

Melinda, Molly, and I were there when the men from the mortuary came to take her body away. They suggested we may want to walk outside, because in their experience removing the body was often the hardest part for grieving families to handle. We knew we wanted to bear witness to this part of my mother's journey, so we decided to stay. But instead of sitting mournfully in chairs as they took her body out, the three of us stood and applauded her, giving my mother a full-hearted and enthusiastic standing ovation for a life well lived.

★ ★ ★

I was feeling the tear in my personal universe from the loss of my parents. My contagious unease manifested in Molly as a desire to move away from the city, to a place much closer to nature. She'd grown up in rural Encino and was always looking for a more rustic place for us to live.

We drove up to Topanga Canyon after hearing about a house that was about to come on the market. Both Molly and I fell in love with it the moment we saw it. I'm not somebody who ruminates for very long—I jump—so, true to form, we decided to buy the house that day. This longtime resident of Beverly Hills was moving to the country.

I spent many mornings hiking our dogs in the 1,600-acre, protected Santa Monica Conservancy parkland that was a short walk up the road from our house. During these solitary walks, I found myself considering what I'd done with my life so far and often I landed on a feeling of gratitude for the entertainment business that had given me so much. I realized that it was time for me to give back in earnest.

I had already been involved with the wonderful work of the Motion Picture & Television Fund, whose guiding principle—"we take care of our own"—is true in ways most people don't even realize.

I had been in the Directors Guild since the 1960s, so I knew what it was like to be part of a guild that was always looking out for their members' rights. I had joined and become vice president of the Producers Guild and had even received the Charles Fitzsimons Award for my commitment to the guild. But Rabbi Omer-man had taught me that being of service was an important part of Judaism. That lesson began to have a deeper resonance for me.

I wanted to do more for the plight of producers. I could do it as an officer of the Producers Guild—and I was participating in that effort—but I knew I could also have an impact if I were elected to be a governor of the Academy, representing the Producers Branch.

In the late 1970s, I had become a member of the Academy. By the early '90s I became very involved in the Producers Branch. I always tried to get nominated as a governor. There was a process that eventually led to four producers being nominated, after which the Producers Branch would vote, and the one winner would become a governor for a three-year term.

Each branch has three governors so that each year one governor either gets re-elected or steps down. If you serve three consecutive three-year terms, you term out and must leave the board for at least one year.

For years I never made it to the top four. Eventually, as my stock rose in my fellow producers' eyes, I started getting nominated as one of the four, but I never got elected to the board.

It's difficult to put yourself out there and then suffer the ego ding of not being elected. My rejections always seemed to sound the alarm that reminded me I would never measure up to my father's achievements. "The Academy was for the big boys" that voice inside told me, but not for me. But I was changing, and that insecurity was never enough to dampen my enthusiasm for the work I loved, so I just kept trying.

I got lucky in 2004 when I was finally elected as a governor of the Academy, a validation that meant the world to me. I joined Kathy Kennedy and Larry Gordon to represent the Producers Branch. I loved—finally—sitting at that table as a governor of the Academy of Motion Picture Arts and Sciences. I have so much respect for our organization that when they invited me to join the board, it had the effect of allowing me to stand a little taller in the world.

43

Even though I had known Mark Gordon for a long time, we became friends when he was part of the retreat group at Kathy's. In 2004–2005 we produced the movie *Hostage* together. In 2007–2008, we produced the Producers Guild Awards shows together and had the kind of blast that solidifies a friendship.

In 2010, when it was time for PGA president Marshall Herskovitz to step down, Mark and I decided to run as copresidents. When we won, we asked ourselves what we wanted to focus on. Even though the Producers Code of Credits was working, we needed to do something else to clarify the actual role of a producer.

While talking to Vance, our executive director, he came up with an equivalent of the Good Housekeeping Seal of Approval. Whoever actually produced the movie would get a p.g.a. mark next to their name, both on-screen and in paid ads. It didn't mean you were necessarily a member of the Producers Guild of America, which was distinguished by its uppercase PGA. What it meant was that it was decided through the guild arbitration system that you had actually done a majority of the functions of a producer as listed in the criteria we'd come up with at Kathy's house years earlier. The arbitration committee would consist of three experienced producers who would look over all the information that the producers provided, as well as third-party testaments as to who actually did the work. It's important that the arbiters remained anonymous. If a producer is not given the mark, he or she may appeal the first arbiters' decision. At that point, two new but experienced producers are added to one from the original group to form the new set of arbiters. Once that appeals arbitration is completed, that decision becomes final.

Our arbitration system was embraced by most of the industry, and the Academy started to defer to the Producers Guild decisions about who could legitimately earn an Oscar nomination.

We had the Academy behind us, which was great, but we also needed the studios to recognize the validity of the p.g.a. mark. It took two and a half years of perseverance and hard work, but eventually, they agreed because—to their credit—they recognized that even though there was no financial gain for them, nor union pressure to do it, in the end, it was simply the morally right thing to do.

By 2014, all the studios had signed on, along with most of the major independents. In 2016, more than three hundred movies were arbitrated by the Producers Guild, and now I'm happy to say that just about everybody wants that little p.g.a. distinguishing mark. We legitimized what a real producer is and ultimately changed the culture.

I was an Academy governor. Not only was I a member of the board, I got elected treasurer—twice—then vice president.

While Mark and I were still working to get the producers' mark standardized, I had become first vice president of the Academy, right behind Tom Sherak. To some people's delight and other's dismay, I had a point of view that I was never afraid to express. I cared.

There began to be moments when I was pestered by a thought that felt like a fly you swat when it circles annoyingly around your ear. Or was it a wish I couldn't let myself entertain? I wasn't sure, but either way, I found myself thinking what had previously been unthinkable: Could I ever run for president of the Academy?

My father had been president in 1977 and while there was a pile of "ifs"—like if I could run and if I could win—a victory would make us the first father and son to be Academy presidents. I was both daunted by and excited about that possibility. Knowing that Tom Sherak would be terming out significantly bolstered my thoughts about running for president.

I talked to Molly, Mark Gordon, Vance, and my buddies Gary Lucchesi, Greg Hoblit, and Michael Manheim. But mostly I talked to myself. I wondered, *Am I willing to stick my neck out this far? Is it possible for a Koch, other than the one named Howard W. Koch, to become president of our Academy?*

While I was going back and forth about it, the one thing that pushed me over the edge into the "Why not give it a try?" camp was realizing that because I'd already been on the board for three consecutive stints, I'd only have one year left before I termed out. It was now or never, so I jumped, knowing that if I won, I'd only have one year to be president.

I asked my friend and fellow board member Phil Alden Robinson if he would nominate me if I decided to run. He thought it was a good idea and agreed to do it.

The day arrived and with it all sorts of dark thoughts, all of which were variations of this one theme: What if nobody votes for me? I arrived at the meeting with my stomach having taken up residence in my throat and utterly unable to eat the hot meal served to us before the meeting began.

The way it usually plays out is that somewhere between three and six people get nominated. A vote is tallied and whoever has the lowest number of votes leaves and then another vote is tallied. This process continues until the one with the majority of the board's votes becomes president.

On this day—the day of learning the true meaning of quaking in my boots—just three of us were nominated. I figured I'd be out on the first ballot.

Each of us was able to make a statement to the board about why we wanted to be president before we were sent out of the room so the board could discuss us, after which we'd be allowed back in to vote with the rest of the governors.

When it was my turn to speak, I told the board that I had been around the Academy since the early 1970s, that I had served on committees for more than twenty years, and that having been at the helm of many motion pictures, along with having been president of the Producers Guild, I felt I knew what leadership was about.

I told the board I felt there were a lot of issues that needed the kind of leadership that I could bring. Having been a producer for many years, I had experience leading large groups of people with goals to meet.

The world was changing, and even though change was hard, I felt the Academy needed it. The board needed to be more open and transparent with its general members. I suggested that one way we could do that would be to have an open membership meeting at least once a year.

I felt we had many branches that were bursting at the seams, and that it was time to look at which crafts should have their own separate branch.

I felt that we weren't paying enough attention to the diversity issues necessary for the Academy.

Lastly, I told the board that were I to win, I would take the year off of making movies and would devote myself entirely to the Academy.

When we'd all spoken, the three nominees walked out of the room and down the hall of the Academy together. There we were in front of the picture of the original organizers of the Academy in 1927. They included Mary Pickford, Louis B. Mayer, Cecil B. DeMille, Irving Thalberg, and Douglas Fairbanks. Looking at those pictures, it was chilling to realize that one of us standing there was going to join that august group as the next Academy president.

We were called back in, whereupon we cast our votes with the rest of the members. Our CFO, Andy Horn, counted all the ballots and after having written down the decision, he handed that portentous scrap of paper to Cheryl Marshall, who was practically an Academy institution herself. Cheryl worked for the executive director for close to forty years; she was the only one who knew what the rest of us didn't know. Cheryl ceremoniously handed the paper to the Academy's outside attorney, John Quinn. Instead of saying what I fully expected to hear, which was, "We're down to two, so-and-so will need to step away," he said the words that I will remember for the rest of my life: "We have a new president: congratulations, Hawk Koch."

Something inside me shuddered when I heard the words that sent a shock throughout my body. I composed myself as best I could, but let me just say that I had never before experienced such an internal physical lurching. I had reached a pinnacle, one that I never really believed I could achieve, and my body was recalibrating itself to make room for the news. Hell had frozen over, pigs had taken wing in the sky, and I had just become President of the Academy of Motion Picture Arts and Sciences. Oh. My. God.

The first thing I wanted to do was tell Molly, but I had to take over the meeting! The moment somebody began to speak for what I could tell would last a minute or more, I reached down into my lap and texted my wife these life-altering words: "I'm prez."

For me, becoming President of the Academy was the equivalent of winning an Oscar. It was the manifestation of the dream I had been afraid to claim as my own. But here it was, here I was, the new president of the Academy.

I felt myself stepping out from under my father's shadow and taking my place beside him. In my imagination, I stood there proudly next to—but no longer obscured by—Howard W. Koch.

44

The very next morning I arrived at the Academy to begin my term as president. I was very aware that I only had a short time to live my dream and I wasn't going to waste a minute of it. Having been around the Academy for over forty years and on the board for eight, I knew what I wanted to do and understood the politics of how to achieve it. Being president was my opportunity to make a difference.

Through all the ups and downs that come with being in the entertainment business, I've never lost my enthusiasm for the ride. I buckle myself in, hold on tight, and go for it. That's what I fully intended to do.

I hung my pictures on the wall to make the office my own. I knew I was in exactly the right spot. Now I just hoped I wouldn't screw it up.

I was very moved by the number of letters and emails of support and congratulations I received—some from people I hadn't seen or been in contact with for many years. One of the first letters I got was from Robert Redford. That was touching to me on so many levels, not the least of which was because we went back so many years.

Once I got settled in, there was plenty of work to do, some of which were changes I wanted to initiate and some of which were related to the day-to-day business of the Academy. Dawn Hudson, our chief executive officer, was a great working partner to me. Dawn had only been at the Academy a year. Prior to that she was the CEO of Film

Independent and helped that organization become a major force in the industry.

In the eighty-five years of the Academy's existence, we had never had a general membership meeting. Our membership had reached seven thousand, so as far as I was concerned, we were way overdue. More than one thousand members showed up in Los Angeles at our Samuel Goldwyn Theater for the first meeting, while hundreds more attended via video conferencing at Pixar in Northern California and others at a location in New York.

We knew it was time for Academy members to vote digitally for the Oscars, instead of using paper ballots as we'd been doing for decades. If we voted digitally, we wouldn't have to turn in ballots until a few days before the Oscar ceremony, giving our members more time to see the films. Additionally, our members would be able to vote instantly from wherever they happened to be in the world.

It's so true that change doesn't come easily. We launched our digital effort during nominations and had so many problems I was ready to abort the mission. I called Phil Robinson and, after explaining all the issues, said, "Phil, I don't know, maybe we gotta go back to paper ballots." He gave me exactly the pep talk I needed. "No, no no no. Don't give up. You can do it. Don't you know someone who could help us?" That's when it occurred to me that I did.

Through my pal Tim Sexton, I had met Craig Schirmer, the man whose company spearheaded Obama's digital campaign in 2008. His expertise was just what we needed. I told him a bit about our dilemma, and he was willing to jump in and help us.

He came in on a Monday morning, looking slightly disheveled, having just returned the night before from Sweden. I could see Dawn was not impressed, but Craig started to talk off-the-cuff and share his ideas of things he thought we could do. They were great ideas! I would learn later that Christina Kounelias, our head of marketing, passed Dawn a tiny piece of paper with these three words she'd written: HIRE THIS GUY! And so we did.

Craig Schirmer is and always will be a hero to the Academy. More members voted that year than had ever voted before. It wasn't an easy transition by a long shot, but we did it, and it's simply how we vote now. We changed an ingrained cultural habit and caught ourselves up to this technological age.

For a long time, the only two events that honored Oscar nominees were the Nominees' Luncheon and the Oscars themselves. I felt the nominees deserved more than just those two celebrations.

At the Oscars, four out of the five nominees for each award go home empty-handed. We decided to honor them by hosting a special dinner for each category, that is, cinematographers had their own dinner as did the sound branch, visual effects, etc. Each branch's nominees could attend, along with their governors. Those governors would invite three icons from their particular branch. For example, the directors' governors invited Francis Coppola, Robert Benton, and Alejandro Iñárritu.

Dawn and I dropped in on each one of the dinners, so we can attest that everyone was having a great time, so much so that those dinners have continued each year since.

Throughout my career, I saw firsthand the contributions each craft made to the final movie, and I knew that without them, the movie would not be the same. That's why it was thrilling for me personally to drop in on these dinners and meet some of the best at their crafts. Most people are in awe when they see a movie star; for me, I was in awe of getting to meet these incredible artists.

Because of their celebrity, the actors had to be handled differently. In their case, I called all their agents and publicists and let them know the Academy was planning something special for their nominated clients. I asked if they would they give me contact numbers and emails for each of them. They weren't happy about it, but they complied. I called each nominee individually and explained that the Academy wanted them to have a great afternoon and luncheon in the company of just the nominees and their governors.

I called my old friend Jane Fonda and asked if she'd host a catered private luncheon at her house for the ten best actress and best supporting actress nominees. I explained that in addition to the nominees, Academy governor Annette Bening would also attend. The idea was that they could come in jeans and flip-flops if they wanted, and just have a good relaxing time in each other's company. Jane thought it was a great idea, and in the end, I think eight of the ten nominees attended, including the youngest award nominee ever, Quvenzhané Wallis, from *Beasts of the Southern Wild*. Jane called me after the lunch and said they had a ball. Wouldn't you have loved being a fly on the wall? I sure would have.

One of the actors branch governors was the well-loved and respected Ed Begley, Jr. I called Ed and asked him if he'd do the same at his house, and he agreed. I offered catering, but Ed insisted on making the meal himself. Again, about eight of the ten nominees showed up and similar to Jane's report, Ed said they too all had a great time. At the Oscar rehearsal later that day, nominee Hugh Jackman, who was rehearsing one of the songs from *Les Misérables* for the show, pulled me aside and said, "I've got to tell you something." "What?" I asked, a bit concerned there might be a problem. "That lunch at Ed's was the most fun three hours I've had in a long, long time."

Another thing we accomplished was getting the board to approve the money to start moving forward on the Academy museum and to undertake the much-needed refurbishing of our home offices.

It was important to me—as it was to a lot of people—that the Academy be more diverse and inclusive. Considering the ways in which we might do that was a constant topic in our meetings.

I felt it was unfair that every craft had its own branch, but the costume designers were combined with production designers and set decorators. It seemed to me the costume designers deserved their own branch.

While all the other branches had three governors, the makeup artists and hairstylists branch only had one. This didn't seem fair either.

Casting directors were included in the members-at-large branch and had been lobbying for many years to have their own branch. I agreed with them.

We were able to accomplish all of these changes in that one year.

* * *

One of the things I was most excited about was getting to participate in the early-morning announcement of the Oscar nominations. It goes without saying that it's exciting to win one, but being nominated is in itself a remarkable achievement. It's the highest acknowledgment given by your peers attesting to the excellence of your creative work.

The day before the announcement, everybody comes to work at the Academy building as usual and at seven o'clock that night, all contact with the outside world shuts down. All the computers, all the IT, and all cell phones are removed. No outside communication is allowed if you're still inside the building at seven. And no outside communication is allowed in—that's how tight the security and secrecy is. Once in, you're not allowed to leave.

After the shutdown, we waited around anxiously for everything to begin. We had some dinner, maybe did a little work to distract ourselves until sometime around nine o'clock, when our accountants arrived.

The accountants handed me a list of all the nominees, because as president, I was the lucky guy who got to see them first. I read the list out loud to everybody, after which the accountants passed out copies so we could all get to work preparing the televised announcement that was scheduled for five-thirty the next morning.

Usually, the president of the Academy is joined by a movie star to read the nominations for worldwide broadcast. I knew that outside the small group of my family and friends, what the public wanted to see were the stars. It was clear that Emma Stone was on the path to becoming a big star, so I decided that she, instead of me, should be the announcer, along with our host for the Oscar broadcast that year, Seth MacFarlane. Around four the morning of the announcement, Seth and Emma arrived and rehearsed the entire list of nominations in the Goldwyn Theater.

After the rehearsal, the press—who had come from all over the world—were allowed in, along with the cameras that needed to be set up and ready by a quarter after five. For a lifelong fan of the movies like me, I was practically bruised from all the times I pinched myself that day at my good fortune.

I hired Neil Maron and Craig Zadan to produce the awards telecast. I thought they were the right team, having produced *Chicago*, *Hairspray*, and *Footloose*. At one point early on they had the great idea to replace the longstanding practice of having a dazzlingly beautiful woman bring out the Oscar for the presenter to hand to the winner. Instead, we held a contest for film students across the country who submitted short films based on this question: How would you contribute to the future of films? Many well-known filmmakers volunteered to look at hundreds of submissions, which were winnowed down to the final six. In addition to having their films on the Academy website, those six film students took turns handing the statuettes to the presenters.

For me there was a very touching moment at the ceremony. Marvin Hamlisch had recently passed away. Having worked on *The Way We Were* and been in the room with Sydney when he first met Marvin, I couldn't help but wonder if Barbra would sing *The Way We Were* during the "In Memoriam." She agreed and paid a wonderful tribute to her old friend Marvin, and to all the others we lost in 2012.

One of the complaints that our Oscar show director, Don Mischer, had mentioned about earlier telecasts was that, other than the actor nominees, there weren't enough celebrities/presenters in the audience to cut away to, because most of them stayed backstage. This is Hollywood's biggest night, and we wanted to be sure the TV audience around the world saw how the stars turned out for the show. I discussed the problem with our Oscar talent booker, Danette Herman.

Danette, who I greatly respect, had been booking presenters for the Oscars for many years. She told the representatives of the celebrities who we were going to ask to present awards that year that they were required to sit in the audience, not backstage. If they didn't agree, they couldn't present. Most of them agreed, so Don Mischer had plenty of cutaways to please the audience at home.

Traditionally, the president of the Academy gives a short speech at some point during the show. I was set to do the same, and I was excited that my whole family would be in the audience. But I was also nervous because, while I'd made a few public speeches before, I'd only made them to a few hundred people at the most. All thirty-five hundred seats in the Dolby Theatre were filled and we were broadcasting to over a billion more. When one of the stage managers came to escort me backstage about fifteen minutes before I was to go on, I was finding it hard to breathe and swallow. My throat was threatening to close up, so I began to summon some ghosts of my past—both in terms of people and experiences—to help me through this moment.

Once backstage, I decided to go outside into the night air and have a go at my own personal scream. Unlike the meek "eh" that was all I could muster with Redford in the desert, this time I allowed myself a full-throated and truly "primal" scream. That letting go had loosened me up, giving me a relaxed confidence.

When I was standing in the wings, I felt my father's presence, as I remembered the year he stood on the stage when he won the Jean Hersholt award. In that moment he voiced out loud for all the world to hear his hope that one day his son would be standing there too. And here I was.

The moment our host, Seth MacFarlane, introduced me, I whispered to myself, "Magic time," and then I walked onto the stage to make my speech.

The nerves were gone, and my voice was strong. I felt fully present and enjoyed every moment. Because I could look into the audience and recognize the faces of people I had known my entire life, I saw their enthusiasm and felt their support of me.

I was happy to dedicate my time on stage to announcing the startup of the Academy Museum of Motion Pictures. Equally meaningful to me was being able to introduce the six film students and their universities.

When my term as Academy president ended, it was bittersweet. I never wanted it to end, but I felt very good about what had been accomplished.

★　★　★

My son Robby had had several girlfriends, but we all knew something was different when he met Annie Meyers-Shyer. They dated for quite a while, but when Annie was ready to make a deeper commitment, Robby, who leans toward the indecisive, couldn't commit. Annie, taking matters into her own hands, broke up with Robby, and soon after adopted a Wheaton terrier she named Wyatt. That did it for Robby, because not only was he in love with Annie, he fell in love with Wyatt too. It wasn't long before they were engaged. Good move, Annie.

Robby and Annie were married in a beautiful ceremony at Annie's mother's home in 2012.

In 2013, my fourth grandson, Theodore (Teddy) Koch, was delivered courtesy of Robby and Annie. While there still wasn't a granddaughter in sight, Teddy Koch brought an entirely new and surprising joy to our family. Two years later, Teddy's little brother, Charlie, was born. That kid seems determined to keep us laughing.

45

I've come to a point in my life where the lessons I've learned (the ones that seem to appear over and over again throughout a long career) have sorted themselves into a list of priorities or tenets. I've been exposed to and involved in entertainment for the better part of six decades. I hope my ability to endure is respectable enough for me to offer some bits of wisdom I've gathered over the years.

HAVE FUN: I mean it. The adage "Life is short" is true. It really is. If you're not having fun in your life, then find a way to change until you do. It goes by way too fast, and it's not worth missing the fun you could be having.

WORK WITH PEOPLE YOU LIKE, BE IN A RELATIONSHIP WITH SOMEONE YOU LIKE: If you're not happy in either your work or your personal relationships, both will suffer. If you're not happy, that's an indication that something needs to change. Let it.

DO SOMETHING THAT MATTERS: Don't go through life expecting everything to come to you. Find the purpose in your life, find what matters to you, and then work toward it. Once you've achieved it, help others achieve it too.

HAVE COURAGE: Most people live in fear. Don't be afraid to make a commitment to what you believe in, to say what you feel, as long as it's done with integrity and consideration for others. You're sure to annoy some people along the way, but you'll be right with yourself, and ultimately, that's what matters most…staying true to you.

LIVE YOUR DREAM: Look deep inside and ask yourself: What is it that I really want to do or be? Who am I? What would you say if you found yourself with only a minute to live, and you're thinking: Did I live the life I wanted to, or did I live the life I thought I was supposed to?

The answer for me would be that for the early (and even some of the middle) part of my life, I lived it as I thought I was supposed to. It took many years, many disappointments, and many trials and errors for me to figure out who I really was so that I could begin to live the life I wanted to live.

My wish for you is that as soon as you possibly can, you heed the sage advice so often attributed to Oscar Wilde: "Be yourself; everyone else is already taken."

EPILOGUE

My father's gifts to me are boundless. He paved the way for me to join his business by opening doors that would likely have remained shut. He opened them for me and then he invited me to walk through them. The moment I did, starting with that first set visit in Durango, Colorado, I knew I'd found where I belonged.

I remember a day sitting at my desk at the Academy after I'd been elected. I was struck by the fact that thirty-six years earlier my dad had occupied the same position I now held. I wondered if when he became president, he missed his dad. At that moment, not only did I miss mine, but I wished he could have seen just how far I followed in his footsteps. I was looking inside myself, taking in this moment, and acknowledging how far I'd come. I had been happily married to Molly for fifteen years, I had three beautiful children, and, as of this writing, I now have five grandsons.

I looked up at the pictures that I had chosen to put on my office wall and saw them as if for the first time. Was that really me on the set of *Chinatown,* and on *The Way We Were,* and on *Heaven Can Wait?* Had I started so far back and continued my fortunate career through *Wayne's World, Primal Fear,* and *Keeping the Faith,* plus all the other movies in between? Did I really get to participate in the making of all those films?

Yes, I did.

It occurred to me sitting at my desk that day that all my life I'd felt burdened by the impossible idea that I was expected to be just like my father. Could I ever be as good, as generous, as thoughtful, or as well liked as he was? No, I couldn't, because I wasn't him; I was me.

I felt a shift in my perspective because I realized sitting there that I was happy with who I had become. I had always wanted to step out from under my father's shadow and stand shoulder to shoulder with him, two individuals in their own right. And finally, I had.

If I were sitting across from the rabbi today and if he were to ask me, just as he did more than twenty years ago, "Who are you?" I would be able to say without hesitation, "I am one lucky man."

ACKNOWLEDGMENTS

I'd like to thank Amy Bookman whom I've known for long enough to trust with my life in words. She added that rare combination of love and ferocity that made for a much better version of this book than it would otherwise have been.

I owe Christina Wool a huge debt of gratitude for reading and correcting umpteen drafts.

I would like to thank the following people for the confidence they gave me to keep going: David Field, Sarah Platt, Mark Gordon, Gary Lucchesi, Lori McCreary, Sid Ganis, Gale Anne Hurd, Dawn Hudson, Robert Evans, Nancy Seltzer, Madelyn Hammond, Joe Veltre, David Gersh, Emily Murdoch Baker, Sam Wasson, Alan and Melinda Blinken, Janice Jordan, Peggy Jordan, Laura Taron, and Julie Bloomer.

I am grateful to the Academy of Motion Picture Arts and Sciences, the Producers Guild of America, and Paramount Pictures, for underpinning my professional life. My hope is that I can give back to you some small measure of what you've given to me.

Debby Englander and Heather King jumped in and calmly shepherded this book to the finish line. Deep bow of appreciation to you.

Whether or not a creative project comes to fruition often boils down to the "yes" or "no" of one person. When it came to publishing *Magic Time*, Anthony Ziccardi said, "Yes." I will be forever grateful.

Molly has given me the strength to keep going. She is my partner on this book and in life. Without her, there is no magic.